the HOLY SPIRIT in TODAY'S CHURCH

a handbook of the new pentecostalism

edited by
ERLING JORSTAD

ABINGDON PRESS
Nashville • New York

THE HOLY SPIRIT IN TODAY'S CHURCH

Library of Congress Cataloging in Publication Data

Jorstad, Erling, 1930-   comp. The Holy Spirit in today's church.
Bibliography: p.   1. Pentecostalism. I. Title.
BX8763.J67   269'.2   73-8691

ISBN 0-687-17293-4

MANUFACTURED BY THE PARTHENON PRESS AT
NASHVILLE, TENNESSEE, UNITED STATES OF AMERICA

Contents

49816

Preface

Perhaps the one movement in recent American church life which is most criticized and defended, yet least understood, is that known as the "new Pentecostalism" or the "charismatic movement." Those who believe in it do so because they know from their own experiences they have received the "charisms" or gifts promised in the New Testament by which they can witness their faith to others. These gifts, similar to those poured out by the Holy Spirit on the disciples at Pentecost, enable them to worship God in new and exciting forms. Many can speak instantly in languages they had not known before; others find the power to heal physical and mental illnesses; still others find the resources to perform other miracles.

Their beliefs and practices are sharply repudiated by a widely varying group of critics who seek to prove such events are understandable purely in human terms. They remember the early years of Pentecostal fervor in the United States as it divided and polarized congregations and denominations into bitterly feuding factions. Rather than find in this new movement a fresh renewal of the charismatic gifts, they fear it is bringing only more rancor and enmity within American church life.

Between its supporters and its critics stand large numbers of Americans who are raising fundamental questions about this movement. It is to this group that this handbook is addressed. What seems most needed at this time is more information about the teachings and the implications for church membership of the new Pentecostalism. Such information will surely not in itself settle the dispute over the movement, nor is such the intent of this book. Rather, the attempt is made first to present a brief historical introduction and then to give the balance of the study to the participants and the critics to speak for themselves.

A word of explanation is needed here as to the basis I used for including some spokesmen and omitting others. Undoubtedly, some readers will feel I omitted a crucial essay or a favorite interpretation. The attempt was made throughout to present those writings which presented as accurately, clearly, and responsibly as possible the major themes of the movement. Within the limits of space, each essay represents the judgments of a substantial portion of those concerned with the new Pentecostalism, be they friends or critics. No attempt was made to omit or to overload any important faction of the movement. The annotated bibliography at the conclusion of the handbook suggests further readings.

Beyond that, one representative selection from the many writings of the nationally known Pentecostalists is included, that being by David Wilkerson. Much of the energy of the new Pentecostalism is involved with his ministry plus those of Pat Boone, Kathryn Kuhlman, and Oral Roberts, other celebrities of the movement. However, their works which are listed in the bibliography at the end of this handbook are readily accessible and need no duplication here. Also, since the movement started around 1960 no writings about it before that date are included, even though this meant omitting so important a foundational study as George Barton Cutten's 1927 book, *Speaking with Tongues: Historically and Psychologically Considered.*

Since most of the questions the general public raises about the movement center on its most controversial themes, this handbook devotes extended space to those issues: Baptism in the Holy Spirit, speaking in tongues, healing, and the presence of demons. These topics are by no means fully representative of new Pentecostal thought, but they are the most frequently and easily misunderstood. Hence the selections on them will occupy more space than on the other Pentecostal teachings.

It is hoped that this handbook will encourage further investigation by the reader and mutual explorations of the questions raised. For that reason, study guide questions are added at the end of each chapter, beginning with chapter 4.

A final word of introduction seems in order here. I first became interested in the movement when doing research on the Jesus people phenomenon and for my course at St. Olaf College on the history of American Christianity. Upon the invitation of my two children, both teen-agers and both very active in the local midweek prayer group, I started attending its meetings on a regular basis. From there I became acquainted with other Pentecostal groups throughout the Twin City and southern Minnesota areas. I have been in correspondence with many of the spokesmen represented in this handbook and have interviewed as many friends and critics of the movement as time and travel arrangements would permit. Perhaps when the readers of this book have completed studying its contents, they will better understand my personal belief that I now better understand the new Pentecostalism but still cannot reach a final judgment on it.

I gratefully acknowledge a generous grant from St. Olaf College for the professional preparation of the manuscript for publication.

1. The First Pentecostalism in America

While historians place the date for the appearance of Pentecostalism in America at about 1900, the participants themselves believe it was founded on the day of Pentecost itself. On that day God revealed his will directly to man for the first time since the ascension of Jesus; hence the directions and the powers given to the disciples on that day represent the oldest and thus the most authoritative understanding of the will of God ever revealed to man. God proved visibly through the powers he poured out through the Holy Spirit on the disciples what he intended subsequent generations of Christians to believe. Thus Pentecostalists believe they must allow the events at Pentecost to guide their every activity as they carry on God's work in the present.

Believers in Pentecostalism recognize that the events of Pentecost, as such, can never be repeated. The "noise like a violent, rushing wind" came from heaven with the "tongues of fire" filling the disciples with the Holy Spirit and giving them the power "to speak with other tongues, as the Spirit was giving them utterance" (Acts 2:2-4). These events were the electricity God was giving them to carry out the great commission to make disciples of all nations. Once given, such powers were ample proof or evidence that God had acted directly in human history and need never again enact another Pentecostal outpouring. The book of Acts recorded what happened; man has only to believe that it did happen.

Pentecostalists believe further that all those who came later to believe in Jesus as their Lord and Savior were given "charisms" or gifts through the event they know as the Baptism in the Holy Spirit. The believers in the postapostolic days down to the present receive at least one, and probably more, of the nine spiritual gifts Paul outlines in I Corinthians 12 from this baptism:

> Now there are varieties of gifts, but the same Spirit. And there are varieties of ministries, and the same Lord. And there are varieties of effects, but the same God who works all things in all persons. But to each one is given the manifestation of the Spirit for the common good. For to one is given the word of wisdom through the Spirit, and to another the word of knowledge according to the same Spirit; to another faith by the same Spirit, and to another gifts of healing by the one Spirit, and to another the effecting of miracles, and to another prophecy, and to another the distinguishing of spirits, and to another various kinds of tongues, and to another the interpretation of tongues. But one and the same Spirit works all these things distributing to each one individually just as He wills. (This is from the New American Standard Bible translation, the one preferred by most Pentecostalists.)

Thus Pentecostalists make the differentiation here between the signs or evidence of the power of the Holy Spirit poured out at Pentecost and the latter gifts of the Holy Spirit given to believers. The latter are to be used "for the common good" to strengthen the faith of the believer and to win converts to the faith. Believers receive these gifts when they accept the Baptism in the Holy Spirit. When the recipient recognizes he has one or more of the nine gifts, he understands he has received a "second blessing," or visible evidence God has sent the power of the Holy Spirit into his life.[1]

The Pentecostal longing for tangible proof that the Holy Spirit was directing their lives might never have taken the turn it did had not its adherents insisted that such proof consist of controversial practices such as speaking in tongues, healing of illnesses, and combatting demons. These activities,

---

[1] See the very helpful discussion in John Thomas Nichol, *Pentecostalism* (Plainfield, N.J., Logos International, 1971), pp. 12-13.

which the Pentecostalists believe have full scriptural authority, produced sharp and often bitter resistance by those Christians who believed such gifts were not truly scriptural and were in fact dividing Christians into hostile factions rather than bringing about the common good.

The controversy over the gifts of the Holy Spirit first broke out in the early church at Corinth. Then slowly but steadily over the early years of the church Christians devoted a decreasing amount of attention to the cultivation of the charismatic gifts of I Corinthians 12. Throughout the history of the church, until the eighteenth century in fact, the record shows that only a tiny number of believers practiced the celebration of the gifts. Pentecostalism, as it is understood in the twentieth century, was a virtually unknown phenomenon for some seventeen centuries of church history.

The first clear signs of renewed interest in what would become Pentecostalism emerged out of the Methodism associated with John Wesley in England in the eighteenth century. He had explored the implications of the doctrine of sanctification—of how a converted Christian could grow in spiritual and moral life. Wesley searched for a clear expression of the resources available to a believer for such growth. These he believed came from the "second blessing," the conviction that spiritual and moral holiness could be approximated if not totally achieved in this life by undergoing a second transforming experience, the Baptism in the Holy Spirit. After the first step—that of conversion—the believer seeking holiness invited the Holy Spirit to dwell in him and bestow on him the additional gifts needed for continued growth in holiness. The physical evidence of possessing such a gift proved to the believer that he had undergone the second blessing and was on his way to holiness.

Wesley's teaching failed to take hold among the majority of Methodists in England or the United States. In the nineteenth century, however, it was discovered by some

Methodists in America who felt compelled to break with the mother church and found separate Holiness churches such as the Church of the Nazarene, the Pilgrim Holiness Church, and the Church of God (Anderson, Indiana).

Almost immediately, however, sharp controversy broke out among Holiness spokesmen over the full meaning of the second blessing. Some insisted it was an instant and complete cleansing from sin, which was demonstrated publicly by vigorous praying, bold bodily movement, and loud shouting. Others believed the second blessing would be proven by some other supernatural sign, such as speaking in tongues. It was from this second group that Pentecostalism in America would emerge.

The supernatural sign did appear to a small group of students enrolled at Bethel Bible College in Topeka, Kansas, headed by Charles Fox Parham. Having studied closely the phenomenon of speaking in tongues, the students were in a highly expectant mood on New Year's Eve, 1900, when gathered for a traditional Watch service. A student, Agnes Ozman, asked that they lay hands on her so she might receive the Baptism in the Holy Spirit. After several entreaties Parham placed his hands on her head and prayed. Later he related:

> I had scarcely repeated three dozen sentences when a glory fell upon her, a halo seemed to surround her head and face, and she began speaking in the Chinese language, and was unable to speak English for three days. Seeing this marvelous manifestation of the restoration of Pentecostal power, . . . we decided as a school to wait upon God. We felt that God was no respecter of persons and what He had so graciously poured out upon one, He would upon all.[2]

That event electrified the student community; now the visible sign had been given. The Pentecostal gift had been given upon the receiving of the Baptism. Parham and some

[2] *Ibid.*, p. 28.

12

of the students soon became traveling evangelists, opening Bible schools throughout the Southwest and holding prayer meetings centering on receiving the second blessing. Their efforts were often met with derision and hostility, but they knew they had been given the power to withstand the forces of their enemies in this world. They continued to preach the Baptism in the Holy Spirit as demonstrated by tongues and healing.

From such urban centers as Los Angeles and Houston the Pentecostal movement attracted steadily growing numbers of members in the next two decades. The leaders found ready acceptance among those who were suspicious or intimidated by the larger denominational churches with formal liturgy and extensive bureaucracies. Those among the "disinherited"—the economically poor or those with little formal education seeking miracles to cure their personal problems —found in the Pentecostal tabernacles the informality, enthusiasm, acceptance, and confidence in the supernatural direction of their lives which they wanted. Across the nation, and with a strong missionary emphasis reaching out around the world, the movement attracted those seeking proof of the indwelling power of the Holy Spirit. Once they had such proof, they no longer feared they would spend eternity in the company of Satan and his demons.

The greatest success in recruiting new members came from the mass meeting in which a celebrity preacher, often with a reputation for healing powers, would speak often for hours at a time. Invariably he or she would bring the audience to an emotional peak with the demonstration of the gift of tongues for those answering the altar call or from the command of the preacher for the sick to be healed. Undoubtedly the most famous early charismatic leader was Aimée Semple McPherson with her tabernacle in Los Angeles in the 1920s.

At the time this growth was taking place, so also was a far less constructive side of the Pentecostal movement emerging. With a deliberate rejection of the kinds of ec-clesiastical authority found in the Roman Catholic Church, or to a lesser degree in larger Protestant bodies, the Pente-costals realized they lacked any final authoritative body to settle the growing number of internal disputes within their ranks. Starting in the 1920s and lasting through the 1950s, Pentecostalist spokesmen quarreled among themselves over the whole range of religious concerns: doctrine, church government, evangelistic techniques, finances, and coopera-tion with other denominations. So bitter did many of these disputes become that by the 20s several large and many small Pentecostal denominations sprang up in all parts of the country. Some included tens of thousands of members, such as the Assemblies of God; others consisted of a handful of congregations in a rural valley. The *Handbook of Denomi-nations in the United States*[3] (Frank S. Mead, editor) shows that before World War II at least twelve separate Pente-costal denominations appeared that could be shown to have extensive membership; it was not known how many splinter groups sprang up and died out during those years. Some of these bodies were exclusively black in their constituency, some were interracial, and some were exlusively white.

This splintering had the effect of convincing each Pente-costal group that it more clearly than its competitors under-stood the meaning of the Baptism in the Holy Spirit and the use of the gifts. Something of a holier-than-thou attitude settled in among most participants as each sought to demon-strate publicly that his body had full access to all the spiritual gifts. Out of this attitude emerged perhaps the most serious weakness of the early Pentecostalism. Members or potential members were told by the contending leaders they would have to demonstrate publicly they had received the gift of speaking in tongues before they could be con-

---

[3] Edited by Frank Mead (5th ed.; Nashville: Abingdon Press, 1970).

sidered bona fide Spirit-filled Christians suitable for membership in the local congregation. This standard obviously led the Pentecostalists to cut themselves off by choice from the major Protestant bodies in the United States and gave the movement an image of exclusiveness based on something as controversial and, to many American churchgoers, as downright weird as speaking in tongues.

Further trouble developed during the 1930s and 1940s when some tiny bands split off from the splinter groups and indulged in such exotic practices as handing around poisonous snakes during meetings to prove God was protecting the handler. Other cults concentrated on frantic emotional outbursts complete with rolling in the aisles, screaming, and hair pulling. None of these were in any way endorsed by the major Pentecostal bodies, but the typical Protestant church member could not help but believe he had no future with such people.

Pentecostalism isolated itself further by its concentrated hostility toward higher education and formally educated ministers. Believing as they did that the Baptism in the Spirit would instantly bestow the gift of wisdom, hence making academic studies unnecessary, most Pentecostal bodies remained content to conduct their services and programs among their own supporters and concentrate on overseas missionary work rather than conduct vigorous evangelism among nonmembers at home. Pentecostalism had drawn into itself, content that it alone through the visible proof of tongues had exclusive access to the indwelling power of the Holy Spirit, making all other Christians something like second-class citizens in the kingdom of heaven. As a result, its influence on mainline American church life was minimal.[4]

[4] See Nichol, *Pentecostalism*, chaps. 7, 8.

2. The New Pentecostalism in the United States

While Pentecostal churches remained isolated from the large denominations in the 1950s, they found new areas for growth and witness. This became especially apparent in two new nationally organized programs, the Full Gospel Business Men's Fellowship International and the ministry of the Reverend Oral Roberts. The FGBMFI emerged in 1951 from the leadership of a California businessman named Demos Shakarian. After several failures in business ventures he consulted with Roberts about founding a Pentecostal businessman's association. His first efforts met with little success until in 1953 he implored heaven for a sign from God concerning his future. He and his wife had a vision given to them in tongues in which throughout the world millions of men, who had seemed dead, "threw up their hands and started magnifying God." [1]

From that day on Shakarian found the direction and momentum to build the Full Gospel Business Men's group. Primarily interdenominational among Pentecostalists in scope, it brought together men from various kinds of business activities who wanted the fellowship of sharing the "full gospel" in settings such as prayer breakfasts, small Bible cell study groups, and weekend retreats. The movement spread abroad and served to carry the enthusiasm of the early Pentecostalists into communities in a more organized fashion than had been done by the older denominations.

The other movement bringing Pentecostalism to the

---

[1] Michael Harper, *As in the Beginning: The Twentieth Century Pentecostal Revival* (Plainfield, N.J., Logos International, 1971), p. 74.

general public in the 1950s was the ministry of Oral Roberts. Born in 1918, he was brought up in the Pentecostal Holiness Church, and became a minister there. He found, in the 1950s, great public interest in his program that he called the Healing Wings Revival Ministry, a well-organized effort to reach out to believers through mass rallies in urban centers. Roberts also made effective use of radio and television and his magazine, *Abundant Life*. Although he drew considerable criticism, hundreds of supporters testified they were cured from serious illness when attending Roberts' meetings.[2]

As popular as these programs were and as fast as Pentecostalism led by Americans was spreading abroad, the major thrust centered on the older requirement that the Baptism in the Holy Spirit be proven by the public speaking in tongues. As a result, no visible inroads were made during the 1950s within mainline American Protestantism.

Historians of the new Pentecostalism agree that the beginnings of that movement came from an Episcopalian parish in Van Nuys, California, in 1960. The rector there, Dennis J. Bennett, had received the gift of tongues and had for several months quietly ministered about the second blessing to members of his parish. About seventy of them came to experience the Baptism in the Holy Spirit themselves. Inevitably, rumors and gossip about these meetings spread through the congregation. Bennett brought the issue into the open in April by reading a letter to his congregation explaining what he understood by the transforming power of the Holy Spirit Baptism and what he hoped it could do for his parish.[3]

However, the divisiveness that had characterized so much of the earlier Pentecostalism now again came to the surface;

[2] Nichol, *Pentecostalism*, p. 224.
[3] The letter is in Harper, *As in the Beginning*, pp. 64-69.

Bennett was asked by his parish leaders to resign to avoid further controversy. The incident was significant because it was apparently the first time an ordained minister in a mainline, highly confessional Protestant body had actively solicited converts to Pentecostalism; and secondly, the incident was given extensive national publicity. It became clear the charismatic gifts were no longer the exclusive property of the "old Pentecostalists."

The new movement emerged rather slowly following the Bennett incident, but it is virtually impossible to trace its subsequent growth with any degree of historical accuracy. This apparent vagueness was soon to become one of the most important features of the new Pentecostalism. While the pattern varied among denominations and individuals, the spread of the movement would usually be along the following lines. An individual, either a prominent layman or a minister in a mainline denomination, male or female, would receive the Baptism in the Holy Spirit. This would be made visible through the gift of tongues, or that of healing, or of prophecy. The resultant joy and assurance of the believer in knowing of the indwelling power of the Spirit would often lead to a visibly transformed personality. The believer would be more enthusiastic about his or her faith, a new concern for the religious life of others would become apparent, and the believer would radiate a joy and inner contentment that had not been present before the second blessing.

The recipient of the gifts would start a midweek prayer group and invite others to share in the gifts. Obviously, not all who attended such meetings were converted to the new Pentecostalism; the attendance and membership, such as it was, varied greatly from week to week. Throughout the 1960s the movement appeared to be strongest among Episcopalians, Lutherans, and Baptists, and to a lesser degree among Methodists, Congregationalists, and Presbyterians. Its impact upon Roman Catholics became visible by the early 1970s (see below, pp. 29-34). Since the movement was so fragmented and varied so much around the country, it is impossible to summarize its impact upon the mainline congregations. From the evidence available, it seems in order to state that some congregations reported more enthusiasm for Bible study and small group discussions and genuine concern for the personal problems of others where the new Pentecostalism took hold. Other congregations found the practice of tongues or healing to be so far removed from their understanding of Christianity that the new movement disrupted and in a few cases broke apart local parishes.

By the early 1970s one solid fact seemed clear about the new Pentecostal groups within the large denominations which had grown so rapidly: that they had continued to grow when they avoided the mistakes made by the older Pentecostal churches of the earlier years. That is, the cutting edge of *insisting* that speaking in tongues be considered the necessary proof of the Baptism in the Holy Spirit was blunted in the new movement. So too was the older Pentecostal suspicion of the medical profession. Most of the new Pentecostalists solicited the aid of both God and their physician for their ailments. By avoiding the demands made by the older groups that an authentic believer must be able to demonstrate publicly his reception of the second blessing, the participants in the new movement could celebrate the charismatic gifts, remain within their own denominations, and not find themselves forced to decide between the two alternatives.

By the early 70s, then, the new Pentecostalism had found the means by which it could avoid the rancor and divisiveness of its predecessor and yet search out within mainline Protestantism and Roman Catholicism those Christians who wanted to experience the second blessing. As it did so, obviously those outside the movement were raising many important and difficult questions about the phenomenon itself. Among the most important was: How many church people really were numbered among the new Pentecostalists? I have been unable to reach any definitive answer to this question, although one minister stated that "eleven percent of the members of the major denominations" had opted for a tongues experience.[4] The membership statistics are unavailable simply because the participants themselves want to keep their movement free from the head counters, who they feel would stifle its openness and spontaneity. To the best of my knowledge, no midweek prayer meeting, the characteristic form of organization for the movement, keeps any kind of membership statistics as would a parish. The participants believe the Holy Spirit can work among two or three in attendance as well as among two or three hundred, and thus they reject any attempt to boast about their movement by heralding its attendance records.

Further, they carefully avoid seeking publicity from the mass media about their movement. They know only too well how eagerly the sensationalistic television or newspaper or magazine reporters flock to meetings where emotions flow freely and strongly and how easily such demonstrations of feelings can be distorted for the general public.

Beyond that, the new Pentecostalism avoids making any concerted effort at organizing leadership for its groups beyond the local level. They prefer each group to go its own way and make little effort to set up metropolitan, regional, or national coordinating committees or councils. Hence, by contrast to the older Pentecostalism, one cannot obtain verifiable information on the individual programs and activities of the members. Most participants carry out whatever

---

[4] See the letter by the Rev. Richard E. Ittner of Oxon Hill, Maryland, in the *Christian Century*, Nov. 29, 1972, p. 1225.

organized church activities they support within their own local congregations and keep their midweek prayer meeting as their personal source of renewal and inspiration. Thus, we may well have thousands of new Pentecostalists in America today, but we cannot demonstrate with any more precision than this handbook exhibits precisely how many there are or precisely what they do outside their own congregations.

Beyond not knowing how many persons are involved, we have no way of knowing in a systematic fashion precisely why they are attracted to this movement. This becomes especially significant when one contrasts the loyalty to certain doctrines shown by the older and the newer Pentecostalists. What seems apparent is that the two groups share the same theology. Both accept the Bible as their sole source of God's will for their life; both hold to a literal, uncritical interpretation of its teachings. Both believe Jesus to be both man and the Son of God, whose substitutionary atonement through the crucifixion and the bodily resurrection assures them of their acceptance into the community of believers who will live for eternity with God. Both believe in the literal bodily second coming of Christ after the resurrection of the dead to judge the quick and the dead. Thus on the rockbed of fundamental doctrine, we detect little significant difference between the older and newer Pentecostalists.

Yet, unquestionably, significant differences are visible, and they are the unique features of the new movement that make it so significant for understanding American church life today. The entire purpose of this handbook, to repeat, is to show the distinguishing features of the new Pentecostalism.

Before presenting the documents illustrating the nature of the movement, it may be helpful at this point to present a summary of what are the most important characteristics of the new Pentecostalism. With the features of the older movement in mind, as well as the acknowledgment of the lack of substantial verifiable information, it seems justifiable to suggest that the following are the distinguishing elements of the new Pentecostalism.

1. The new movement almost unanimously chooses to remain within it own denominational membership rather than joining established Pentecostal bodies (such as the Assemblies of God) or starting new groups.

2. With some exceptions most new Pentecostals do not require public speaking in tongues as proof of being baptized in the Holy Spirit.

3. A considerable number of the new group come from different social, economic, and educational groupings than the old. Most of the new come from upper-middle-class, well-educated backgrounds, being college graduates or college students.

4. The midweek prayer meeting is enthusiastically opened to anyone who wants to attend, regardless of any prior denominational affiliation.

5. Some new Pentecostalists have established communal living arrangements, sharing households and incomes.

6. All the new groups make their meetings as informal as possible concerning dress, prior planning of the program itself, and remaining open to minister to the personal needs of any in attendance who ask for help.

7. The level of emotional expression is one of joy and celebration, but firmly controlled against excess display.

8. By contrast to the older Pentecostalism, which usually involved itself heavily in overseas missionary support, the new movement focuses primarily around the interests and needs of the local group. Those interested in missions show their support by working through their local congregation.

9. The new movement makes a more vigorous outreach to teen-agers and young adults.
10. The older moral code prohibiting any members from smoking, dancing, using make-up, and the like, is absent in the new Pentecostalism.
11. In today's movement many more women are actively involved as leaders.
12. Finally, the new Pentecostalists follow the established liturgical order when worshiping in their own congregations, rather than the older Pentecostal practice of spontaneous contributions at any given point. The new participants cultivate the "Spirit-led" services at their midweek meetings.

Undoubtedly, other differences could be listed here. This list of twelve, however, constitutes the general national expression of the new Pentecostalism, while unique local customs may well prevail about which I am uninformed.

New Pentecostalism, as just defined, has met opposition from most shades of the theological perspective, radical to conservative. Surprisingly, even though the conservatives share several decisive doctrines with the new Pentecostalists, they are by comparison more critical and often suspicious of the movement than their more liberal colleagues with whom they share far fewer theological convictions. Thus, in the next chapter we will briefly consider the principal objections to the new Pentecostalism as it has emerged in the last dozen years. Then we will be in a better position to understand and evaluate the actual writings from within and outside the movement itself.

3. Controversy over the New Pentecostalism

That sharp controversy within the churches over the new Pentecostalism should emerge after its appearance is not surprising. Like rapid and controversial change in any field (such as education or politics), the participants in the new movement forced the leaders and laity within existing churches to respond to their new life in the Spirit.

Since this phenomenon is still very much alive and growing today, it is impossible at this date to make an accurate and full assessment of the sources and kinds of opposition it has produced. However, one striking feature is clear; contrary to what many observers might think, the criticism is far more sharp and sustained from the more conservative and fundamentalist wings of Christendom than from the more moderate and liberal groups. This is surprising because on the surface the new Pentecostalists and the fundamentalists seem to share so much: (1) unquestioned belief that the verbally inspired Bible is the sole and inerrant source of knowledge of God's will for man; (2) vigorously defended local autonomy over the control of the congregation as opposed to any more centralized ecclesiastical bureaucracy; (3) a strong emphasis on simplicity and informality in worship service; and (4) conscious efforts to give the laity as much power in group matters as possible. Father Kilian McDonnell has said that while Roman Catholics are altar-centered and Lutherans are pulpit-centered, Pentecostalists of all varieties are pew-centered.

However, many of the more conservative and fundamentalist elements are in sharp disagreement with the movement.

First, many conservative church groups have their own mid-week (or Sunday evening) prayer meetings. These are obviously open to the general public but are attended mostly by the local parishioners. Hence they find little need for an additional midweek meeting such as the new Pentecostalists conduct.

Second, as will be discussed in more detail below, the conservatives fear that the teaching and practice of Baptism in the Holy Spirit and the speaking in tongues will seriously disrupt and most likely break apart their own theology which rests on the belief that the Christian faith can be clearly defined and understood by precisely stated doctrines. The new Pentecostalism is, to them, too spontaneous and open to acceptance by personal experience than by their cherished loyalty to the propositional doctrines they find expressed in the Bible. This loyalty to doctrine is, in turn, the result of the conservatives' long and often acrimonious debate with more liberal theologians and church spokesmen from the early twentieth century who also believed, as do Pentecostalists, that the essence of religious faith could not be expressed in logically constructed doctrines.

Third, although little evidence on this point appears in print, it seems that the conservatives fear the new Pentecostal manner and principles (hermeneutics) of interpreting the Scriptures. Pentecostalists are judged to go to the Bible to find proof texts for what they already believe about the second blessing, while the conservatives insist their own method of interpretation is to let the Scriptures lead them wherever that direction might be without prior commitment. This theme is fully developed in the books by Anthony A. Hoekema, Merrill F. Unger, and Frederick Dale Bruner listed in the bibliography (pp. 157-60).

Fourth, conservatives and fundamentalists have had considerably more experience in this century with itinerant faith healers, revivalist ministers, and free-lance preachers than have the members of the mainline denominations, where new Pentecostalism is the strongest. Thus, it seems, the former are simply more cautious, even suspicious of those who now almost overnight claim to have miraculous new powers of healing, tongues, prophecy, and the like. One has only to recall the kind of exploitation of fundamentalist audiences exposed in the movie *Marjoe* to understand why they today are less enthused over miracle workers.

Fifth, since all forms of Pentecostalism believe in letting the Holy Spirit move the church group concerned, conservatives fear that they cannot control such energy by the more traditional means of decree and established church program. They are accustomed to working through established ecclesiastical channels rather than following the Spirit into new and untested realms. Church leaders characteristically are searching for new forms of increasing the religious life of their people, but they usually stop far short of putting full confidence that the Spirit will lead them no matter what.

Finally, many conservatives join with liberals in concluding that many of the more controversial new Pentecostalist practices are understandable almost exclusively in human terms, generally as seen and interpreted by psychology. Both groups of critics agree that Spirit-filled Christians are not necessarily more neurotic or unbalanced than those without the spiritual gifts. But both are agreed that new Pentecostalists are more susceptible to hypnotism, the influence of an appealing leader, and the influence of lively music and shared prayer than are nonparticipants; hence their convictions are really normal, human phenomena rather than the direct supernatural work of the Holy Spirit. (See in the bibliography the works by Hoekema and John P. Kildahl.)

Given all these general considerations, what specific objections are raised? The following is a broad listing of these;

specific criticisms of specific new Pentecostal teachings are presented in the body of the text.

Most often, most church people fear that the new movement will become as divisive as the old. Some, such as Campus Crusade, have gone so far (as seen nationally in the well-publicized Explo '72 program in Dallas) as to forbid any expression in tongues or planned discussion of them. Others, such as Billy Graham and his associates (see the books of Leighton Ford, Sherwood Eliot Wirt, and John Wesley White) preach on the power and the filling by the Holy Spirit but stop short of discussing Baptism in the Holy Spirit.[1]

Beyond the divisiveness church people fear that the Holy Spirit Baptism, tongues, healing, and prophecy too often bring the recipient a sense of pride, even arrogance, over the gifts he now has but that are not the possession of those outside the charismatic experience. Morton T. Kelsey in *Tongues Speaking* makes the point (seconded by Hal Lindsay in *Satan Is Alive and Well on Planet Earth*) that teaching that the Baptism is an instant experience often leads to the confusing idea that slow, steady growth is unnecessary and that the new gifts can lead the believer in short-cut fashion to full religious maturity.

Virtually every critic from every theological tradition agrees that the second blessing is simply not necessary. Once a person is converted to accepting Christ as his personal Lord and Savior, there is no need to go beyond receiving the personal assurance of salvation. (See below, for a full discussion, pp. 71-76.) Almost all critics agree also that tongues especially, and probably the other gifts of I Corinthians 12, were given for a specific need at a specific time and that their further issuance from God stopped after his

---

[1] For a superb example, see chap. 8 of *Jesus Power* (New York: Harper & Row, 1972), by Sherwood Eliot Wirt, editor of the Billy Graham Evangelistic Association monthly paper, *Decision*.

purposes at that moment were fulfilled. In other words, since only a tiny handful of Christians spoke in tongues after the apostolic age and before the Bethel Bible College experience, it is safe to assume, they believe, that God no longer was giving this power to Christians.

Regarding demons, exorcism, and healing, many critics fear that the new Pentecostalists will fall into the trap of blaming all their own troubles and the illnesses of mankind on demons who can be conquered only by exorcism—laying on of hands and the like—rather than by common sense, modern medicine, and continued prayer life.

Finally, critics agree that since new Pentecostalists admit that speaking in tongues is not indispensable proof of receiving the powers of the Spirit but is certainly the *normative* sign, such a teaching creates unwarranted tension and worry among many who go form one meeting to another hoping to receive the Baptism in the Holy Spirit there. Not believing they have received it, the critics suggest, they begin to have serious if not neurotic doubts about the state of their spiritual health. As a result, they may well give up in despair and in the end show less interest in religious faith than before they began their quest.[2]

However, new Pentecostalists have heard these criticisms for over a dozen years now and are prepared with answers. Their positions, plus the most responsible, detailed criticisms of the movement, will constitute the balance of this handbook. The study guide questions hopefully will help sharpen the issues to lead the reader to his own decisions.

[2] Anthony A. Hoekema, *What About Tongue Speaking?* (Grand Rapids: William B. Eerdmans Publishing Co., 1966), pp. 78-79.

4. The Midweek Prayer Meeting

Perhaps the best way to introduce the new Pentecostalism is to present the reactions of a nonmember who attended the prayer meetings.

The following selection is by Peg Meier, a staff writer for the Minneapolis Tribune, *who reports on a Catholic charismatic meeting she attended. Such meetings are typical of many throughout the larger cities in America.*

Pentecostal Rites Stir Catholics*

An hour before the Thursday prayer meeting is to begin, they start to trickle into the basement meeting room. A middle-aged woman carrying a Bible. A bearded young man wearing jeans. A nun in habit. A business executive type. An elegant woman wearing a pants suit. A tough-looking man.

The trickle of people down the church steps becomes a steady flow, and by 8 P.M., more than 600 people are gathered for a Catholic Pentecostal meeting at St. Albert the Great Church, 28th St. and 32nd Ave. S.

They seem to know each other, and they can pick out strangers to welcome them.

Three young people with guitars start the meeting by strumming a song. It has overtones of folk music. Most of the people know the words, and the room is filled with joyful singing:

> All of my life,
> I will sing praise to my God.

* From the October 22, 1972 issue; reprinted with permission of the *Minneapolis Tribune*.

> For creation praise;
> For salvation praise;
> For all mankind praise.

There are requests for favorites in the song book—some traditional hymns, some new songs. "Holy God, we praise Thy name." "The Lord is a great and mighty king, just and gentle in everything." "He touched me."

Then silence, silence that seems impossible in a room crowded with hundreds of people.

Next to you, there is a woman in her 30s praying, her hands covering her face. You notice a faint murmur and you realize it's the sound of many whispered prayers. A man's voice, from somewhere rows in front of you, begins singing. Maybe it's chanting. The words are indistinguishable. Then you understand—this must be "speaking in tongues."

A hand is slowly lifted above the seated audience. Then its mate is lifted, and more hands reach out for the Holy Spirit. The murmur grows in volume. Almost a buzz. Occasionally you can make out a phrase: "Praise Him, praise Him, praise Him" seems to come from behind you. "Oh Jesus, Oh Jesus," you hear. Handkerchiefs are dabbed against eyes. There is audible weeping.

The voices seem to be dying out. The hum is becoming softer. There has been no signal for the prayers to end, as there was none to begin. It seems spontaneous.

A leader of the Pentecostal movement (or charismatic renewal, as the participants prefer to call it) steps to the microphone. The people are sitting on folding chairs in circles around him. He explains the meeting to people who are attending for the first time.

"Many people ask what is a prayer meeting," says Jack Brombach, a social worker by training who is now a full-time counselor to the Catholic charismatic community. "I

like to explain it as coming to know Jesus in a deeper way.
. . . It's to receive grace, to be uplifted, to be encouraged."

Brombach tells of scriptural and historical background
of such prayer meetings. He speaks of Paul's letter to the
Corinthians, in which the apostle told them not to suppress
the gift of tongues. He reads from the Book of Acts and
recounts stories of early Christians gathering together for
daily prayer.

"Let's really lift our hearts and our tongues to Jesus,"
Brombach concludes. The murmur of prayers begins again.
It ends with a strong male voice singing "Alleluia" and the
group joins in the song.

Someone says from his chair, "Thank you, Jesus." Another
person from another part of the room says, "Thank you for
all our blessings." About a dozen more thank you's are
uttered: "Thank you, Jesus, for taking care of the little
things." "Thank you for the gift of motherhood." "Thank
you, Jesus, for setting us free."

There is a 10-minute address from the Rev. William
Farrell, a full-time priest with the charismatic community
who is known as Father Bill. He tells of the beauty of living
a life with Jesus "when we are constantly given His free
grace, His life, His constant presence."

And there is witnessing from the audience: A woman in
a brown dress thanks the group for praying for her 83-year-
old mother, the victim of a stroke a month ago. The woman
said prayers had returned her mother's speech and the doctor
said she could go home from the hospital.

A blonde girl, of about college age, said she has learned
to take her problems to her "true Father" in heaven, rather
than running to her earthly father whenever she "gets
harassed."

A nun in a blue suit tells of her joy since she learned to
trust Jesus and feel His nearness.

More singing. Prayers. An invitation to offer to each other

31

"a piece of Jesus Christ"—hugging, shaking hands, greetings of "the peace of Jesus to you."

The people are asked to contribute what they can to support Brombach, his family and the movement. One of the coordinators says, "I've found I can live better on 90 percent of my income, giving 10 percent to the Lord, than I can on 100 percent. It's a mystery. But it works."

Hundreds of people stay after the two-hour prayer meeting for coffee and cookies. People linger in the church until midnight, asking "prayer teams" for guidance or just talking.

Unusual for the Catholic Church?

Not any more—even Catholics are feeling the effects of the current wave of evangelistic fervor which generally is associated with Protestant fundamentalists. Leaders of the renewal movement estimate that as many as 20,000 Catholics in the nation are involved.

The growth has been recent. The first national convention of the charismatic organization within the Catholic Church in 1968 was attended by 100 people; the 1972 meeting attracted several thousand.

Although the initial reaction of American Catholic bishops was one of astonishment and skepticism, the movement has received at least their cautious endorsement since 1969.

In an interview after the Minneapolis meeting, Brombach said the crowd of 600 was small. Usually there are 800 or 900 people, he said. He guessed that 75 or 80 percent of the participants are Catholic. Many are priests and nuns, some in clerical garb and some in street wear.

Prayer meetings and the other elements of the charismatic movement are not intended to replace the Mass, liturgy, sacraments or other traditional parts of the Catholic faith, Brombach said. As far as reaction goes from the church's hierarchy, he said, "The bishop knows we're here." That doesn't indicate enthusiastic approval, he said, but neither does it indicate rejection.

Of the usual 800 people at a meeting, about 400 are regulars, another 200 or 300 come and go and another 150 or so are first-timers, Brombach estimated.

"The first time people are here," he said, "they tend to be embarrassed, confused or scared. Many come out of curiosity and are prepared to laugh. But it's strange—sometimes they come again because they see a group of Christians who really love each other. And they find that the praying does something for them."

Praying in tongues is a small part of the charismatic movement but the part that creates the most puzzlement among newcomers. Brombach defined it as the Holy Spirit entering the body to join with the spirit in praising God. (A person attending the meeting defined it as "praising God in languages I never learned but which the Holy Spirit gave me.")

Those who have studied the sounds of speaking in tongues say it is usually unintelligible, yet it has the patterns of vocabulary and inflection which resemble human language. Some Pentecostals say they have spoken in tongues and learned later that they were speaking an actual language, but one not familiar to them, such as an archaic form of French or Bantu.

Healing is also a part of the movement. In the Minneapolis group, there have been cures of measles, strep throat, torn ligaments—"no great big major type of healings but blessings, nonetheless," Brombach said. God sends these blessings to people who have accepted Him totally and who ask for His help, Brombach said, not to those who seek Him out just for a quick cure.

The Thursday night prayer meetings are four years old, and the group has outgrown several meeting places. (The present meeting place at St. Albert's Church is rented; the group is not affiliated directly with the church.)

Brombach doesn't like to talk about crowd size: "We

are growing in numbers. But more important, we're growing in depth."

An outgrowth of the prayer meetings is a community of 48 adults and about the same number of children "who have made a covenant together." Living in three households, the community prays together several evenings a week and "share our lives," Brombach said. "It's like an early Christian community."

People who attend the Thursday prayer meetings are eager to tell of the changes in their lives.

Pat McAlpin, a 39-year-old insurance agent from Columbia Heights, said he was raised Catholic, went to a Catholic college, married in the church and trained his seven children in it. But something was missing in his faith, he said. Charismatic renewal provided something new in the past six months.

"Our lives have blossomed," he said. "There is more peace in our home and love for one another. The warmness we feel here is carried home."

Conrad Pena, 22 a factory laborer who plays guitar during meetings, said he and his wife, Chris, were in spiritual difficulties. They had tried drugs and yoga and had experimented with the occult. Then they found Jesus in the charismatic movement.

"Since we found Him, He's changed our lives completely and we praise Him for it," he said.

The Penas live in the charismatic community. Mrs. Pena said Jesus so completely rules there that she was even trusting Him to let her know what to prepare for a Saturday community dinner.

Beyond the large, urban-based prayer meeting just described, the new Pentecostals attend a wide variety of other kinds of such events. This variety is in marked contrast with the more formalized meetings of the established Pentecostal denominations. The following selection outlines briefly the main concerns and types of meetings. The author is an active lecturer and writer for the charismatic renewal.

Varieties of Prayer Meetings*

Preparation

Prayer meetings have to be prepared for. They don't just happen. I'd like to talk about the ways of preparation. The first and most important way of preparation is the individual prayer lives of the people who are there. If a prayer meeting becomes dead and lifeless, very often it's because the individual people do not have a deepening personal contact with God. And if you find problems cropping up in your prayer meetings, one of the sources of these can be the lack of personal prayer and contact with God in the individuals there. Growth in private prayer is essential for the growth of a community in a prayer meeting. And what should really happen in prayer meetings is that each individual has come in a spirit of prayer, having prayed each day during the week, walking more and more in close contact with God so that what happens in the prayer meeting is that this prayer just surfaces. Not that it began for the first time since the last prayer meeting, but rather the prayer, the spirit of prayer, the centeredness on the love of God that's there already surfaces at the prayer meetings. And so one very important part of the preparation for a prayer meeting is the personal, private deepening in prayer of each individual person.

Another part of preparation is prayer specifically for the prayer meeting, and especially for the leaders of the prayer meeting. Each person before coming should pray for the success of the prayer meeting and for each person coming.

* Jim Cavnar, *Prayer Meetings* (Pecos, N.M.: Dove Publications, 1969), pp. 25-27, 3-5, 33-35.

And the third thing in the way of preparation is that people should come to prayer meetings more immediately prepared too, in two ways: 1) They should come prepared to receive whatever God wants them to receive. They should come with hearts prepared to receive whatever God wants to give them. They should come with minds open to receiving from God what He wants. They should come, in a way, like sponges ready to soak up all that God wants to give. 2) Even more importantly, they should come with something to give, they should come primarily out of their love for their brothers and sisters and come mostly because they want to do whatever they can to their brothers and sisters and to strengthen them. They should ask God beforehand in their own private prayer, and then again at the prayer meeting, "What should I do tonight? Should I bring a scripture passage to share? Should I tell them about this incident in my life? Should I share this thought you've given me? What should I bring? What can I bring? What will You give me to bring to share with my brothers and sisters?" We should come to prayer meetings in a spirit of charity, self-sacrificing charity, that seeks above all the love of the brothers, and above all to give to one another, to strengthen one another. If prayer meetings become quiet and dead and lifeless, very often it's because we're not coming in love, we're not coming primarily to see what we can do to help and encourage one another.

Various Kinds of Prayer Meetings

I want to tell you a little bit about some of the various prayer meetings I've seen. Last summer I was out in California and Steve Clark took me over to the house of a man named Paul Larson. Paul and his wife were there, and Ed Gregory, whom some of you know, and Mel Boring and his wife and another woman. They were sitting around the dining room table when I came in and sat down. I thought it was a prayer meeting. During the course of our talking, the lady who was there was telling us about having received the gift of tongues the day before. And then they asked us to tell what had been happening at Notre Dame, so Steve and I described the things that had been happening there and I told a little bit about what had been going on in my own life. And while we were still speaking Ed said, "Jim, why don't we wait a minute; I think the Lord wants to speak to us." So there was silence. And then there came a very strong prophecy. And after the prophecy, very naturally, there began to grow out of the group a murmured prayer of praise to God, then breaking into singing in tongues which just welled up out of the whole group. I'd never heard singing in tongues before; but it was real praise of God, everyone singing different words and melodies, but all blending together in harmony and building on one another. Then it died down and there was a little murmur of prayer and we continued talking and praying and at the end, just before Steve and I left, we prayed together. They came around and laid hands on us and prayed over each one of us and a number of prophecies came forth about our lives and our futures—prophecies which (to my surprise I must admit) seem to be borne out. And that was a prayer meeting.

While we were also in California we went to a place called Faith Tabernacle, which is a non-denominational center. There were about 500 people there and David DuPlessis was speaking. When we walked in there were about 500 chairs arranged semi-circularly about the stage of a huge auditorium. It began with people praising God, with their hands lifted up—all these hundreds of people with their hands lifted praising God, with many people praying in tongues. And then singing in tongues began, even in that large group; and this was the beginning of the whole thing, what you might call a prayer meeting—all these people praising God with uplifted hands. Then there came forth a message in tongues from someone in the group and the pastor who was on the stage gave the interpretation. And then there was more prayer, and I believe that at one point there was another message in tongues and another interpretation. Later David DuPlessis spoke and after the meeting people began to go off to various rooms. In one room off to the side people were receiving the baptism of the Spirit; in another room people went for prayer. And this was a kind of prayer meeting. And during the whole thing the pastor was much more of a leader than, say, in the prayer meeting in the Larson home. And from moment to moment he led and told what to do, saying, "Now, let's do this; now let's introduce our speaker," and after David spoke, "Let's have a prayer in thanksgiving to God." And if a message came in tongues with the interpretation, he might say, "Because of this message let us join hands and pray together." One could have been there more like a spectator, though it wouldn't have been very easy to have kept from joining them.

At Estes Park, Colorado, where I was about a month and a half ago, Inter-Church Team Ministries was conducting a conference with about three prayer meetings a day; about 130 people were there. And they would usually begin with the leader getting up and saying, "Let us begin now with prayer of praise and worship." And people would begin to pray and someone might lead out in a prayer aloud, and then someone might lead a song, just beginning and everyone would take it up, and then someone else might lead another song, and everyone would take that one up and it would die and then another song. And in between the songs a murmur of prayer going on among all the people. And then singing in tongues would well up from one part of the group and spread over the entire 130 people and then sort of die down and then maybe another song, or maybe some more prayer, maybe prayer aloud. And then in the context of this worship of God, this constant worship and praising of God in English and in tongues and song and every other way, prophecies would come forth and sometimes the whole course of the meeting would be directed by the prophecies. One night we stood for about a half an hour and there were about 15 prophecies that came forth one after another and sort of painted out a unified picture of what God was doing among his people with exhortations to prayer coming through these prophecies. And one could just tell, I could just tell, when the Holy Spirit would say, "Now let's do something else," and the leader would get up and introduce a speaker who would be there that night to speak, maybe a long thing, maybe very short, maybe two or three people would have short things to share. And then the whole thing would end with some kind of prayer together and conclude with a song. And these prayer meetings would last anywhere from an hour to three hours, with 130 people joining in that kind of worship and prayer together.

Some Problems

1) Don't seek publicity. Publicity will usually come, but don't seek it. Seek only God and growth in his love, and when God wants he will bring publicity. But great harm can sometimes be brought about by seeking publicity.

2) Don't focus on the devil. Confrontations with Satan will arise and they can be dealt with as they do, but one of the greatest mistakes that a prayer group can make is beginning to focus on Satan too much—demon-hunting. Focus instead on worship and scripture, upon the love of God, and when confrontations with Satan must be dealt with directly they will be taken care of. But focusing on Satan can undermine a prayer group.

3) If there is deadness in a prayer meeting there are usually causes. Many times what will be needed is that people come prepared to give something. Other times it may be the lack of private prayer or apostolic action in the lives of those coming. Leaders can talk to the members of the group and suggest that they come with something to give and urge them to greater faithfulness in private prayer and apostolic action.

4) If a prayer meeting consistently becomes too much of a discussion and ceases to be a real prayer meeting, there are things that can be done to overcome the difficulty. One thing is more private prayer for the prayer meeting. Another thing would be for the leader to suggest "waiting on God," that is, that the group at the prayer meeting just remain silent, waiting for God to speak through spiritual gifts or to move someone to speak or read a passage from Scripture. "Waiting on God" means really trying to wait for the action of God in the prayer meeting, really putting it into His hands and speaking only what He gives us to speak, saying nothing on our own but only as He urges and approves.

What It Is Leading Us To

Remember the prayer meeting I described at the Larson's house during the summer? Well, that wasn't a prayer meeting. It was just the normal gathering together of Christians. At one time they had been having many prayer meetings each week, but the Holy Spirit began to lead them to have only one a week and instead to rely on Him to bring the people together in His way for prayer. And so it will happen, as it did that day, that people will come over because they felt drawn by the Spirit and a group will spontaneously gather and prayer will spring up naturally and freely. As someone is fixing dinner a message in tongues may come forth. In the middle of a discussion a prophecy may come forth that will lead to prayer and singing in tongues and worship. A spirit of prayer and worship has begun to fill their lives at all times until all of life has become a prayer meeting. This is what God is leading us to: to so live with Him and with one another that our whole lives will become a prayer meeting.

Perhaps the best known new Pentecostal leader nationally among young people is David Wilkerson, founder of "Teen Challenge," a rehabilitation program for urban young people involved in drugs, crime, or alcohol. Among the many ministers working among inner city youth, Wilkerson drew his inspiration from new Pentecostal theology and practice. The following selection is indicative of his approach to the problem and is, in its own way, a representative example of a new Pentecostal-type meeting.

The Holy Spirit in the Inner City*

The boy's name was Roberto. Roberto was sixteen years old; he had been on heroin for two years, and on marijuana before that; he had been in jail four times, once for stabbing another gang member in a street fight. The boy had lived, but Roberto was afraid that some day he might kill. Unlike many of the boys who come to the [Teen Challenge] Center, Roberto had parents who stood by him. They tried everywhere to get help, but Roberto's downhill slide only increased its pace.

That afternoon I met Roberto in the chapel. I guessed from the way he was fidgeting and moving around restlessly that he was about to go out for a fix.

"I've got problems, Davie," he said, quietly lacing and unlacing his fingers. When an addict says he has problems,

* David Wilkerson, *The Cross and the Switchblade.* Chosen Books, Inc., distributed by Fleming H. Revell Company, Old Tappan, N. J., pp. 161-64.

he means he has to make contact and shoot it up—and soon.

So I started talking to Roberto again about the baptism of the Holy Spirit. "Nicky [Cruz, author of *Run, Baby, Run* and Wilkerson's most famous convert] will be preaching about it tonight. Be there, and let the Spirit come upon you."

"I don't know, David. I've got to get some fresh air. I'm not feeling so good."

I had to let him go, and frankly I didn't expect to see him again. But that night he was in the chapel when I arrived. I could tell from the way he continued to suffer that he had made it without getting a fix. I sat down beside him, and watched him carefully as several of our ex-gang members and drug addicts arose and quite simply told of the wondrous things that were happening to them. Nicky preached about the need of every drug addict to have the baptism in the Holy Spirit.

"If you want power in your life, . . . if you are on the needle and really want to change, then listen to this. The Holy Spirit is what you need. And when you receive Him, you will also receive ten special gifts which you can depend on. I'm going to tell you about them. If you have a pencil and paper you can copy down the Bible references that show where I got them.

"First of all you have power. You can read that in Acts 1:8. You shall have power when the Holy Spirit comes upon you.

"Then, you're going to have a Comforter. John 14:26. A Comforter doesn't mean someone who will make you comfortable, it means someone who will stand by you and give you strength.

"Next, you will have protection. Read in Acts 16:6 how the Holy Spirit forbids the apostles to take a step which would have been tragic. He will guide you like this, too.

"And here's an important one: you will no longer be hounded by the mind of the flesh, but you will have spiritual values. Read it in Ephesians 2:3-6.

"You will have life. Now you are headed for death, but with the Holy Spirit, it says in Second Corinthians 3:5-6 that you will have new life.

"And you will be living with the Spirit of Truth. The needle holds out a promise to you that is never fulfilled. You don't get release in a drilling session, it just gets worse. John 16:13 tells you that you will have Truth.

"Access to the Father will be yours. Read Ephesians 2:18.

"And the last three: You will have Hope. How many of you have that now? Not many. You will have Hope, says Romans 15:13.

"And the point of all this is found in Second Corinthians 3:17. You, you boys out there now, will have liberty!

"And how does this come about? Through a dramatic, sudden, overpowering experience. Read about it for yourselves in Acts 10:44."

Then Nicky stopped. His voice dropped and he spoke in almost a whisper. "That's what's ahead for you in this new life," he said. "But here tonight I don't think we want to *read* about it. And we don't want to *talk* about it. We want to *do* it!

"If you want this change and power and hope and freedom in your life, get on your feet and come up front. I'm going to lay my hands on your head just like St. Paul did and the same thing is going to happen to you that happened to the new Christians in his time. You're going to receive the Holy Spirit!"

Roberto took one look at me and leaped to his feet; and my heart leaped with him.

"I want everything God has for me," he said. "I want to make it through and never come back."

Roberto fairly ran to the front of the chapel. He grabbed

43

Nicky's hands and put them on his own head. Almost immediately the same thing happened to this boy that had happened to my Grandfather; he began to tremble as if current were flowing through him. He fell to his knees, and the other boys stood around him, praying.

It was like reliving a scene fom the Book of Acts. In less than two minutes a new language was flowing from Roberto's lips. It poured out like a spring bubbling up out of dry land. Of course, everyone was rejoicing. All the other drug addicts came around Nicky and Roberto and began saying, "He's going to make it. He's coming through." Nicky kept saying, "Thank you, Lord. Thank you for helping these boys." Then others picked up.

"Thank You, Lord. Thank You for helping these boys."

"Thank You. Thank you. Thank You, Lord."

One of the most important but least known elements in a new Pentecostal meeting is the "tarrying meeting." Although it has various expressions, its principal scope is well described here by a minister who early in the new Pentecostal movement received the Baptism in the Holy Spirit. Since then he has been a bridge between its recipients and his church body, the American Lutheran Church (ALC).

This is a hitherto unpublished letter, written to me in response to my question about the nature of the event. The letter has a direct, personal quality, unencumbered by academic refinements, which gives it a sense of immediacy which is so characteristic of the phenomenon he describes. The term "tarrying meeting" comes from Luke 24:29, "Tarry ye in Jerusulem" (AV), interpreted here to mean to wait for God to act.

The Tarrying Meeting*

The tarrying meeting is where the action takes place. It is here where people ask for, and often receive the Bap-

* Letter of Pastor James H. Hanson, Trinity Lutheran Church, Crookston, Minn., to Erling Jorstad, January 29, 1973; used by permission.

tism of the Spirit and the sign of speaking in tongues. It might also be in the tarrying meeting where a person who seems to be blocked from receiving this gift might have prayers of exorcism said over him. It is the private meeting [Editor's Note: taking place after the general public prayer and praise meeting]. It is the meeting of initiated with those who wish to be initiated.

The content of the meeting is usually direct action. Someone will request the laying on of hands and there will be prayers for healing or for the gift of tongues or exorcism or whatever. It is not as programmed as the first part of the meeting. Sometimes in the tarrying meeting, you might find experiences that seem to be excessive in emotion, and somewhat frightening to the uninitiated. I have mixed feelings about the tarrying meetings. At the present time, the involvements that I have had here in Northern Minnesota have not included tarrying meetings.

The reason for the tarrying meeting is that for many of these people the experience of receiving the gift of tongues is something that seems to require a willingness to almost address themselves emotionally. One of my good friends who received this gift in Montana said to me one day, "Jim, it is sort of like having to take your pants off in public." His feelings may not be shared by all people, but I could be sensitive to this.

Most of us would like to know what is going to happen. We know when we go forth to receive the bread and wine in the Lord's Supper that we go in faith, and we are to open our mouths and receive the bread and wine, and we are to eat and to drink. It isn't that frightening an experience to us. However, if we really thought about the content of the Lord's Supper, and what is being given to us, we might have different feelings. However, when it comes to receiving the gift of tongues, most of us have little or no conditioning for this, unless we were to mentally project oursleves into situations where we expressed verbally but not in language that is rational or articulate. I think of the kinds of yells that might come forth from the crowd at an athletic event—hurray! hurrah! Sis-boom-ba—or some of the songs that we used to sing around the campfire when we pretended we were African natives and sang in something of a kind of gibberish. It was fun to do and filled a kind of emotional need and sort of tickled our spirits.

The other setting, in which we might mentally or emotionally place ourselves in order to receive this gift, would be something like the feeling of a child, or as we are trying to identify with our children who are speaking to us in sounds long before they can speak English. In other words, the attitude seems to be one of child-likeness and this becomes our starting point. Many folks, and I was numbered among them, found this to be particularly difficult, because we wanted to be able to receive a Spiritual gift, but wanted to use normal, rational processes that we identify with the learning process, rather than becoming more primitive. It may be precisely at this point where John Kildahl [1] might be right in saying "that this is a learned experience, it is taught." Very seldom have I seen someone spontaneously move into speaking with tongues without some kind of "coaching."

Many of my brothers and sisters in the Charismatic Movement chafe under the title of coaching or chafe at the use of the phrase "coaching." I do not chafe at it, because if someone had not coached me, I would not have received this gift. And I don't see anything wrong with coaching. Coaching simply means placing the person in the kind of emotional and spiritual environment, and the kind of direc-

[1] Editor's Note: he refers here to the book by John Kildahl, *The Psychology of Speaking in Tongues* (New York: Harper & Row, 1972).

46

tions that make it possible for him to appropriate a gift from God. We certainly do not hesitate to coach our children in praying their table prayers or their night time prayers. We do not hesitate at being taught or coached on how to pray in a group or to offer sentence prayers in a group, or whatever. And there is always that kind of embarrassment when we are breaking into something that does touch our spirits and our emotions. So, this is why, I believe, tarrying meetings have come into being. And I would encourage you, as you seek further information and more of this dimension of the Spirit, that you attend some of these sessions. I would encourage you to be of an open mind. I would also indicate that staying for the tarrying meeting does not necessarily mean that you must ask for any of the gifts.

I think that the whole area of understanding the word "gifts" needs some tremendous study in terms of the church. We talk of the "gift of preaching," and yet we know the number of hours which a man spends in taking public speaking, and exegesis and New Testament theology, etc., before he is "qualified" to exercise the "gift of preaching." We also talk about the Sacraments as being "gifts," and yet there is a good deal of training and understanding involved, and certainly much coaching, even as to how we are to approach the altar in some of the more orthodox churches.

So I have no fear of the use of the word "learn" or "coaching." I think that they are perhaps not inappropriate words. But having been coached and trained, so to speak, to speak with tongues, the spiritual effect on myself was enough so that I could say, "Yes, this is the gift of the Holy Spirit; this does warm my heart toward God, this does cause me to direct my thoughts toward God; and to read with relish and joy the Holy Scriptures."

Study Guide Questions to Chapter 4

1. Why might a new Pentecostal prayer meeting produce such differing reactions among observers?
2. What specifically Pentecostal doctrines help shape the form of the prayer meeting? Why is it different than the vespers or matins of the large Protestant denominations or the Catholic Church?
3. Do you think that coaching as described here is too forced a manner for helping people receive the Baptism in the Holy Spirit?

5. The Bible

The Pentecostalist knows his experience of the charismatic gifts is God's will because it harmonizes with the biblical teachings on this subject. Hence, the Bible is seen by all members of the movement as the final authority on all doctrinal matters. They further believe that to use the gifts according to God's command, and to be fully prepared to share this understanding at the midweek prayer meeting, they must spend considerable time alone reflecting on the Bible.

The two selections, one by a Lutheran minister and the other by a Catholic layman, indicate the general approach to the devotional life. Bryne's selection serves as a useful bridge to the next chapter since it outlines a program of prayer for those searching for the Baptism in the Holy Spirit. Christenson's advice assumes such an experience has already taken place.

The Rev. Larry Christenson was one of the first mainline Protestant denominational pastors to introduce the charismatic gifts into his congregation, Trinity Lutheran Church, San Pedro, California (American Lutheran Church). Further reflections by him are found in his more recent book, A *Message to the* Charismatic Movement (*Minneapolis: Bethany Fellowship Dimension Books, 1972*).

How to Have a Daily Quiet Time with God*

One of Jesus' parting commands to His disciples was this: "Make disciples of all the nations" (Matt. 28:19). The word "disciple" comes from the same root as the word "discipline." A disciple is not just a curious or casual follower of Jesus, but a disciplined follower. This is what Jesus wants us to be.

To achieve something worthwhile always requires discipline. No person ever mastered a musical instrument with-

* Reprinted by permission from *Speaking in Tongues,* by Larry Christenson, published and copyright 1968, Bethany Fellowship, Inc., Minneapolis, Minnesota 54438.

out the discipline of regular practice. Every athlete submits to rigorous disciplines in order to excel in his chosen sport. A lawyer, doctor, housewife, mechanic, secretary, student, engineer—each must follow prescribed disciplines in order to excel. Isn't it reasonable to believe that we must also follow spiritual disciplines to excel in a profession, a sport, a hobby—which prepare us only for this life—shouldn't we much more follow strict disciplines which prepare us for eternity? No discipline will pay greater dividends. "The things that are seen are transient, but the things that are unseen are eternal" (II Cor. 4:18).

The Christian religion is essentially an experience—a personal experience of God. Theology and doctrine are simply an explanation of that experience. Many people know something about the doctrine, but have never really had the experience. So of course their religion is dry, formal, powerless. It has no life, no zest, no sense of reality. "This is eternal life, that they might know thee, the only true God, and Jesus Christ whom thou hast sent" (John 17:3).

The simple discipline suggested on the next pages can change all that. It can lead you into a living experience of God. It is a daily quiet time with God. Every great Christian has followed a discipline similar to the one suggested here. No Christian can afford to bypass this basic spiritual discipline. It is gloriously simple. Yet it is astonishingly effective. We challenge you to put it into practice faithfully for one month. Even in that short time you will see the potential it has to literally change your life. "For the word of God is living and active" (Heb. 4:12).

What Do I Need?

1. A Bible.
2. A notebook (preferably a small loose-leaf which you can carry about with you).

3. A pen or pencil.
4. A quiet place.
5. A definite time set aside each day—at least 15 minutes to begin with. (It can grow to an hour!) The early morning is usually the best time. Make it the same time each day, whenever possible.

What Is the Procedure?

1. Realize that God is with you in your quiet time. He stands ready not only to meet with you, but actually to guide and direct you. "When the Spirit of truth [the Holy Spirit] comes, he will guide you into all the truth" (John 16:13). How does God come to you? He comes to you principally through His Word, the Bible. This is the channel which the Holy Spirit uses most frequently.
2. Begin with a brief prayer. Thank God for His special blessings to you and for being here with you now. Tell Him that you believe—you are expecting—that He will meet with you, speak to you, and reveal His will to you through this quiet time. "You will seek me and find me; when you seek me with all your heart. I will be found by you, says the Lord" (Jer. 29:13, 14).
3. Read the brief passage of Scripture which you have chosen for the day. (See Scripture suggestions, page 141.)
   a. Do not read simply to "understand." Read with a feeling of "openness" and "receptivity." You are "feeding" on God's Word. It is spiritual food to you. "Man shall not live by bread alone, but by every word that proceeds from the mouth of God" (Matt. 4:4).
   b. You will not understand everything you read. Don't let that bother you. Take it in. Whisper to God,

51

"I don't get all of this . . . but I know that You will help me to understand as we move along." "The fear [reverence] of the Lord is the beginning of knowledge" (Prov. 1:7).

c. Let your reading be broken up by moments of prayer and meditation. In other words, enjoy this spiritual meal. Taste it. Savor it. Read parts of it out loud to hear how it sounds with differing emphases.

4. Write down what comes to you during this reading-meditating-praying time. THIS IS THE KEY TO YOUR WHOLE QUIET TIME. When you write down, you begin to crystalize and capture the actual workings of the Holy Spirit in your heart, mind, and soul. Make it quite personal and direct. Not simply what the passage "means," but what it means to and for you. Perhaps it will trigger some thought not directly related to the passage you are reading. That's all right. Write it down. This is the Holy Spirit's personal message to you.

a. Naturally you are not always "tuned in" to the Holy Spirit 100 percent—you will get some "static" from your own thoughts and opinions. But more and more, as you faithfully follow this daily discipline, your little notebook will become a record of God's personal dealing with your own life.

b. Here is an actual sample of someone's quiet time record for one day: "June 3rd. The Lord's Prayer. The Apostles' Creed. Romans 6:22-23. Now that I am set free from sin and become a slave if God, my return is sanctification and its end, eternal life. For the wages of sin is death, but the free gift of God is eternal life in Christ Jesus, our Lord. It's a good feeling to rid ourselves of sin, to feel clean and in God's good graces everlastingly. How can we know and learn of God without the will to do so? This I think of so much of late. But what joy it brings to know we have our heavenly Father, our living God, to go to. We give thanks to Thee, yes, more than thanks, O Lord our God, for all Thy goodness. Amen."

5. Close with a time of prayer.
   a. Begin with thanks, praise, adoration.
   b. Confess your sins, asking God's forgiveness.
   c. Affirm your faith in God. Say at least several strong statements of faith. For example—"God is my refuge and strength! . . . I know that Jesus Christ is alive, and His Kingdom is surely coming; it will come to me today! . . . I can do all things through Christ who strengthens me! . . . With God nothing shall be impossible! . . . The Lord is my shepherd! . . . He leadeth me, O blessed thought!"
   d. Present to God your petitions and requests. You may want to keep a prayer-list, and check them off as God answers them. Don't be satisfied with unanswered prayer. Jesus said, "Whatever you ask in prayer, believe that you are receiving it and you will" (Mark 11:24). Keep the list small enough so you can pray for each need with real purpose and faith.

Other Points

1. A Daily Quiet Time with God is one spiritual discipline —one of the most important—but still only one. If your life as a Christian is to mature in a healthy way, you will want to observe other basic disciplines as well. These can be carried out most effectively within the framework of your own local church:
   a. Regular church attendance.
   b. Regular Bible study under a qualified Bible teacher.
   c. Regular giving to the Lord's work (ten percent of your income).

    d. Regular work or service for the Lord under the supervision of those placed over you in the Lord.

2. Divide your notebook into two sections. The first section is to record your Daily Quiet Time. In the second section you take notes on sermons, lectures, Bible studies, radio talks, thoughts that come to you during the day—anything of spiritual value. In order to integrate these notes into your life in a practical way, convert them into a prayer during your next quiet time. In other words, take the substance of the notes and boil it down into a prayer. Apply it to your own life.

Where Should I Start in the Bible?

1. One of the simplest methods for selecting your daily Bible passage is to read through a single book, a few verses each day. The Gospel of John, Colossians, the Epistle of James, and the First Epistle of John are good ones to begin with.

2. You may want to follow certain themes, such as salvation, forgiveness, healing, etc. If so, use a Bible concordance to find different passages dealing with your theme.

3. Another way to begin would be to use the following series of Bible passages, which will lead you through some basic Christian teachings in a systematic way. Some can be covered in a single day; others might be worth spending several days on:

    a. The "new life" of a Christian. I John 5:9-13, James 1:2-8, James 1:19-26, I John 1:5-10, Mark 8:34-38, Eph. 2:1-10, I Pet. 1:3-9, I Pet. 1:22–2:3, John 15:1-11, II Cor. 5:14-21.

    b. Christian responsibility. Phil. 4:4-13, I Pet. 3:8-17, Rom. 14:13-23, Col. 3:16-25, Gal. 6:10.

    c. Adventuring in the Psalms. Psalms 1, 8, 73, 32, 46, 139, 91, 22.

The author is a graduate of Notre Dame University and serves as coordinator of the Notre Dame Charismatic Community and director of the Communication Center and the National Conference of the Catholic Charismatic Renewal. He has traveled extensively throughout the United States on behalf of his community and has written extensively about it. This selection indicates the confidence a charismatic has in the ability of the Holy Spirit to indwell the true seeker.

Scriptural Meditations Preparing for the Baptism in the Holy Spirit*

These meditations are suggested as a program of daily prayer for those seeking the baptism in the Holy Spirit. The readings from scripture have been selected to provide a basis for this quest. It is important, though, to approach the readings *in faith*. If we approach the word of God in humility and faith, he will instruct us through it (cf. II Tim. 3:16-17). For this reason we encourage you not only to follow the recommended format, but also to make these meditations with your heart and will, as well as your mind. Let the word of God dwell richly in your heart.

How to Begin

1) Times: there are three daily meditations. They follow a unified theme and are listed so as to build upon each other. Plan to spend three 10- to 15-minute periods each day in meditation. It is important to make this an explicit commitment and to keep it faithfully. Let this be your sign to the Lord of how serious you are about his Spirit. It is not enough, though, to just "put in" this time; in the midst of a busy schedule, you should probably begin by recollecting yourself. Recall God's living presence. Recall his good-

---

* From James Byrne, *Threshold of God's Promise: An Introduction to the Catholic Pentecostal Movement* (Notre Dame: Ave Maria Press, 1972), pp. 53-55.

ness and mercy and make an act of faith in him. It is quite helpful to withdraw into a different physical location—where possible, a chapel or church is preferable. The first period should begin as soon as possible after rising in the morning. The second can take place during the afternoon or early evening. The third should precede retiring for the day.

2) If at all possible, *speak aloud*. Say the prayers, read the passage aloud, and, if helpful, reflect aloud upon the passage. Conclude by praying aloud. (If this suggestion does not prove helpful, disregard it.)

3) 4 steps:

    a. *Pray* to the Holy Spirit. Begin each meditation by inviting the Holy Spirit to teach you. Recite the prayer to the Holy Spirit. Let the words come from your heart. "Come Holy Spirit, fill the hearts of your faithful and kindle in them the fire of your love. Send forth your Spirit and they shall be created. And you shall renew the face of the earth. Let us pray: O God who by the light of the Holy Spirit did instruct the hearts of the faithful, grant by the same Holy Spirit we may be truly wise and ever rejoice in his consolations. Through Christ our Lord. Amen."

    b. *Read* aloud the passage indicated.

    c. *Reflect* upon the passage. Ask yourself what the passage said. Compare this to what you know about God. Ask what it has to say to you in your situation.

    d. *Thank God* aloud in your own words for his presence and his love. Close with an Our Father.

PASSAGES

Day 1—Jeremiah 31:31-34 and Jeremiah 32:37-41; Ezechiel 37:1-14; Joel 2:28-32 (in most bibles); in Douay-Confraternity versions, Joel 3:1-5

Day 2—Luke 1:5-17 and Luke 1:39-45; Luke 1:26-35 and
    Luke 1:46-55; Luke 2:22-35
Day 3—Mark 1:1-8; Matthew 3:13-17; Matthew 11:7-15
Day 4—Luke 4:14-21; John 3:1-15; John 4:7-26
Day 5—Luke 24:13-49; John 14:22-27 and John 16:1-15;
    Luke 11:9-13
Day 6—Acts 2:1-21; Acts 2:22-42; Acts 10:1-48
Day 7—Acts 22:1-21; Romans 7:14-25 and Romans 8:1-
    17; Acts 19:1-7

Study Guide Questions for Chapter 5

1. How does this program of Bible study differ from your
   own?
2. With their reputation for joyful public celebration, of
   what value to the new Pentecostalist would be so much
   emphasis on individual, quiet reflection?
3. After reading the selections in Chapter 7 on speaking in
   tongues, look for similarities between that and Christenson's suggestion to write down what the Holy Spirit is
   saying to the reader. Is it possible one could write in
   tongues?

6. Baptism in the Holy Spirit

The doctrine and practice of the Baptism in the Holy Spirit give Pentecostalism, in its old and new forms, its unique character within Christianity. Without it, there simply would be no Pentecostalism; with it, the Pentecostalists are convinced they have the miracle-working powers of God through the Holy Spirit as the evidence of their faith.

Because this doctrine and its attendant practices are so important, and because they are so controversial among non-Pentecostalists, this chapter presents an extended discussion of the issues involved. One brief word explaining my system of organization is needed here. Almost all Pentecostalists organize the nine gifts discussed in I Corinthians 12 into three categories:

> Gifts of Inspiration
> > *Tongues*
> > *Interpretation of Tongues*
> > *Prophecy*
> Gifts of Revelation
> > *Word of Knowledge*
> > *Word of Wisdom*
> > *Discerning of Spirits*
> Gifts of Power
> > *Faith*
> > *Healings*
> > *Miracles*

However, the reader will notice in the following chapters I give much more attention to tongues, discerning of spirits, and healing than to the other gifts. This is done simply because these gifts are the ones most misunderstood by the general public and by the participants themselves. I am not suggesting, by the amount of space devoted to these gifts, that I am proposing a rearrangement of the order of gifts.

What the selections in this chapter attempt to do is (1) define the doctrine, (2) describe its personal impact on its believers, (3) explain its meaning in some detail and, (4) present the most responsible criticism of it by theologians.

Don Basham, an ordained minister in the Christian Church (Disciples of Christ), is a full-time writer and lecturer on the new Pentecostalism. This selection is an excellent brief description of the Baptism in the Holy Spirit.

Holy Spirit Baptism*

What is the baptism in the Holy Spirit?

The baptism in the Holy Spirit is a second encounter with God (the first is conversion) in which the Christian begins to receive the supernatural power of the Holy Spirit into his life. Jesus promised this power to his disciples when he said,

> You shall receive power when the Holy Spirit has come upon you and you shall be my witnesses in Jerusalem, and in all Judea and Samaria and to the end of the earth— Acts 1:8.

This promise was fulfilled at Pentecost when the Holy Spirit fell on the one hundred and twenty gathered in the upper room.

> They were all filled with the Holy Spirit and began to speak in other tongues, as the Spirit gave them utterance —Acts 2:4.

This second experience of the power of God, which we call the baptism in the Holy Spirit, is given for the purpose of equipping the Christian with God's power for service. It is the spiritual baptism from Jesus Himself, in which He begins to exercise His sovereign possession, control and use of us in supernatural fashion, through the Holy Spirit.

By way of illustration let us point out that the New Testament describes two baptisms for the believer; baptism in water and baptism in the Holy Spirit. In Matthew 3:11, John the Baptist says,

> I baptize you in water for repentance, but He who is com-

* Don Basham, A *Handbook on Holy Spirit Baptism* ($1.00). Available from Whitaker Books, 504 Laurel Drive, Monroeville, Pa. 15146.

ing after me is mightier than I. . . . He (Jesus) will baptize you with the Holy Spirit and with fire.

In Acts 1:4-5 Jesus says,

For John baptized with water but before many days you shall be baptized with the Holy Spirit.

And in his first sermon, preached on the day of Pentecost, Peter tells the multitude:

Repent and be baptized (water baptism) for the forgiveness of your sins, and you shall receive the gift (baptism) of the Holy Spirit—Acts 2:38.

According to Scripture, these two baptisms are indicative of two separate, major experiences of the power of God. The first is conversion; the sinner's acceptance of Jesus Christ as Lord and Savior which brings salvation. He (the repentant sinner) gives testimony to his response to the gospel and his acceptance of Christ by receiving baptism in water for the remission of sins. Here we see the new believer as the object of God's redemption. But the Lord is not satisfied with our conversion alone; He has promised us power to be His witnesses. So, a second time we are confronted with the power of God; this time in the baptism in the Holy Spirit through which the Christian is brought into a deeper relationship with Christ and the Holy Spirit for the purpose of making him—not an object, but an instrument of redemption.

The two baptisms may be compared as follows:

Christian Baptism by immersion in water

1. The candidate: the pentient believer (Matt. 28:19, Acts 2:38).
2. The baptismal element: water (Acts 8:36-38).
3. The baptizer: man—a preacher, evangelist, deacon (Acts 8:38).
4. The purpose: a witness to conversion and the remission of sins (Acts 2:38, Acts 22:16).

5. The result: salvation and entry into the body of Christ (Mk. 16:16; Gal. 3:27).

Baptism in the Holy Spirit

1. The candidate: the baptized believer (Acts 2:38, Acts 8:14-17).
2. The baptismal element: The Holy Spirit (Mk. 1:8).
3. The baptizer: Jesus Christ (Matt. 3:11, Mk. 1:8).
4. The purpose: to endue the Christian with power (Acts 1:8, Lk. 24:49).
5. The result: reception of the Holy Spirit with accompanying gifts and powers (Acts 2:4, Acts 8:14-16, 1st Cor. 12:4-13).

Why is the baptism in the Holy Spirit so important?

Jesus considered the baptism in the Holy Spirit so important that he expressly forbade his disciples to begin their ministry until they had received it. He knew it was essential for them to have the power which baptism in the Holy Spirit provides.

And while staying with them he charged them not to depart from Jerusalem, but to wait for the promise of the Father, which he said, "you heard from me, for John baptized with water, but before many days you shall be baptized with the Holy Spirit"—Acts 1:4-5.

There are many reasons why the baptism in the Holy Spirit is important. Rufus Moseley listed the following reasons in a little pamphlet entitled, "The Gift of The Holy Spirit."

(1) It is only through this Heavenly gift empowering us, guiding us, and transforming us that we have immediate union with the glorified Jesus and are given power to do His work and His will and to grow up into His likeness. As blessed as was the ministry of Jesus in the flesh, and as glorious as was His redemptive work in Gethsemane and Calvary, and His ministry during the resurrection appear-

61

ances, all this was preparatory to what was given to Jesus with power to impart when He ascended into the presence of the Father, and took His place upon the throne of the universe.

(2) If Jesus had remained on earth until now, with all His power to heal everyone He touched and everyone who touched Him, and had continued to perform all His mighty miracles, He still could have been only at one place at a time. People in their sefishness would have run over each other to get to Him. But since He went into glory and received the gift of the Father with power to share it with those who believe and obey, He has become omnipresent. Moreover, He has power not only to be with His disciples always, giving them what to say and what to do concerning everything they need to do unto the end of the world, but also power to come within and reproduce Himself in terms of all the capabilities of each one of us. Now He can give Himself totally to each one of us without neglecting any of the rest of us.

(3) Through ineffable union now, open to every believing and obedient disciple of Jesus, every one of us finds himself on the opposite kind of a cross from His. He was put upon a cross of shame; we, through happily yielding and responding to Him, are put upon a cross of highest honor. He was put upon a cross of agony; He puts us upon a cross of bliss. He was put upon a cross of death; He puts us upon a cross of life. When Jesus hung upon the cross of shame and agony and desertion, He gave up the Holy Breath or Holy Ghost; when we are put upon the cross by the Holy Spirit we receive the Holy Breath and are filled with the Holy Ghost.

(4) The Holy Spirit is the only Consciousness that knows Jesus and is capable of revealing Him as He is. All human philosophies and theologies tend to whittle Him down to fit their own molds. The Holy Spirit changes us to fit the heavenly mold.

(5) The Holy Spirit, by revealing Jesus as He is, at the same time reveals us as we are. We are convicted of sin and incompleteness by seeing His sinlessness and perfection. As we see ourselves as we are, and see Him as He is, and make the acknowledgment, the miracle of forgiveness and cleansing and transformation occurs. He does not leave us in our nakedness; He furnishes the covering. He does not condemn us; He comes to our rescue. As we only know the mistakes in mathematics by knowing mathematics, it is only by knowing the truth that we can correct the mistakes. So the knowing of Jesus reveals the sin and the lack, and at the same time cleanses us and makes us whole.

(6) It is through the Holy Spirit that we are guided into all truth and shown things to come and given power to overcome (John 16:13).

(7) Through the gift of the Holy Spirit, the body becomes consciously the Lord's. Here it is realized that the Lord is for the body, and the body is for the Lord. We become not only spirit of His spirit, mind of His mind, and soul of His soul, but we also become bone of His bone, flesh of His flesh, hands of His hands, feet of His feet, eyes of His eyes, ears of His ears, tongue of His tongue and everything of His Perfect Everything. The body will never feel as it should as long as it feels itself. As the body is for the Lord and the Lord for the body, the body only feels as it ought to feel when it is feeling the Lord, and the Lord is never happy about the body except in having charge of it and imparting to it the health and the blessing of His presence.

Many other reasons for the importance of the baptism in the Holy Spirit could be listed. Others will become apparent as you read further in the book.

Is baptism in the Holy Spirit essential for salvation?

No, baptism in the Holy Spirit is not essential for salvation. Salvation, or conversion, or the acceptance of Christ as

Lord and Savior is a separate, prior experience. Millions of Christians who love and serve Jesus Christ as Savior have not received the baptism in the Holy Spirit. The New Testament makes it plain that baptism in the Holy Spirit is a second work of grace which follows conversion.

> Philip went down to a city of Samaria and proclaimed to them the Christ. . . . But when they believed Philip as he preached good news about the kingdom of God and the name of Jesus Christ, they were baptized.
>
> Now when the apostles at Jerusalem heard that Samaria had received the word of God they sent to them Peter and John, who came down and prayed for them that they might receive the Holy Spirit; for it had not yet fallen on any of them, but they had only been baptized in the name of the Lord Jesus—Acts 8:5, 12, 14-16.

At times baptism in the Holy Spirit may come immediately following conversion, like in Acts 10, when Peter preaches to the household of Cornelius. On that occasion as Peter preached faith in Christ and forgiveness of sins through His name (Acts 10:43), those who heard, believed, and were immediately filled with the Holy Spirit (Acts 10:44-48).

Peter's statement in Acts 2:38 seems to indicate that baptism in the Holy Spirit should immediately follow water baptism. While this may be ideally true and occasionally happens today (a missionary friend related how young converts in Mexico came up out of the baptismal waters praising God in tongues and prophesying) it is not common. Most Christians today receive the baptism in the Holy Spirit only after instructions and specific prayer.

Again, let us state that while we know the baptism in the Holy Spirit to be an important Christian doctrine, and a vastly needed Christian experience for bringing New Testament power back into the church, it is not essential for salvation.

The author here being interviewed is considered the first mainline Protestant denomination minister to introduce the charismatic gifts into his congregation's life. He continues his ministry in the Episcopalian church as well as writes and lectures on this subject. His definition is included here because it clears up the misunderstanding many noncharismatics have about what "baptism" means to the Pentecostal.

Holy Spirit Baptism*

Q.: What about such ministries as "laying on of hands?" A.: We do not go around laying hands on people with the idea that we will thus impart the Holy Spirit to them; we just pray for the Holy Spirit to be stirred up. The minister can instruct. He can make sure, for instance, that people are willing to forgive others, that they want to receive Christ and are willing to forgive others, that they want to receive Christ and are open to the Spirit. But we cannot give them the Holy Spirit. We do everything we can to offset the idea that we are imparting something. There has been a tendency to confuse the "rite" of baptism of water with the baptism in the Spirit, whereas the Greek term for baptism can mean "identification with," and "overwhelming." Jesus said, "You will be baptized with the Holy Spirit." I like to translate this: "You will be flooded with the Holy Spirit."

The manner in which the Baptism in the Holy Spirit is received varies widely among converts. The following account describes how a group of college students experienced the second blessing. The journal in which the selection is printed is published by the group sponsoring this meeting, Campus Fellowship, with headquarters in Waco, Texas.

* From "Dennis Bennett: Mainline Charismatic: An Interview," by Mirium Murphy. Copyright 1972, Christian Century Foundation. Reprinted by permission from the September 27, 1972, issue of *The Christian Century*.

Baptism in Water*

December 27-30, 1970 found several hundred students from all over the United States, Canada, and Mexico gathered in Waco, Texas, for a mid-winter Campus Fellowship Conference. For four days the Spirit of the Lord rained down joy and love. Complete strangers became close brothers in the Lord. Girls, who had never met before, wept, prayed, worshipped, and sang together in that close fellowship and acceptance of one another that can be precipitated only by the Lord. Above all, the presence of the Lord hovered over the entire meeting like the mighty benevolent cloud that led the Hebrew children out of bondage.

One of the most moving experiences of the conference was the baptism of forty-six young people at Lake Waco. Boys and girls alike walked out into the cold water, following in the footsteps of Jesus. In the wondrous way that never fails to amaze, radiant and joyous Christians came up out of the water praising the Lord, hugging one another and shivering in the winter wind. Praise the Lord, not one developed a cold!

Though warmer than usual for late December, the day of the Baptism service dawned gray and overcast. All the way to the lake, clouds obscured the sun, but when the service began, the sun came out as a shining sign of the blessing of God.

Another wonderful evidence of the loving hand of God was apparent when the soaking wet group climbed back into the big bus. It had come down from cold Minnesota, and was equipped with extra heaters in front and back. The bus, filled with singing Christians wrapped in blankets, carried a traveling prayer group back to the Grace Gospel campground.

The Baptismal service itself was a wonderful example of

* *Campus Fellowship*, Spring, 1971, pp. 1, 2, 14, 15.

the moving of the Lord in the hearts of those attending the conference. At the first service, ten people asked to be baptized. Following a study with group discussion on baptism, twenty-five wanted to be included. When the bus was ready to pull out, nearly fifty were candidates, and a large group of fellow brothers and sisters in the Lord had gathered to observe the service. . . .

[Editor's note: These six students attended the conference at Waco and told of their receiving the Baptism in the Holy Spirit.]

Bill McAlpine, Westmore College, Le Mars, Iowa. I am a religious sociology major. I am studying for the ministry in the United Methodist Church. Next year, I am going to seminary. School can be very trying with a lot of pressure connected with your social life and constant pressure about grades. The Lord has given me a peace of mind about school. I found this very important.

Ellen Dick, Oklahoma City, Oklahoma. The Lord is blessing me by helping me to walk in the spirit instead of the flesh and today as I was baptized in water, the Lord cleared my sight. My eyes were pretty bad, but they are getting better and I am trusting the Lord. I was baptized in the Holy Spirit on New Year's Day last year. There is a feeling like there is a river inside just flowing continually. It is something you really cannot explain.

Craig Brandt, St. Olaf's College, Northfield, Minnesota. The Lord blesses me every time I have fellowship. He opens the heavens and lets down his blessing. During this conference He opened a new realm in speaking in tongues showing me how glorious it is to talk to the Lord God. Actually I had spoken in tongues before I had the "laying on of hands," but I did not know what it was. It was a complete experience that I had on my own.

Marcia Mohr, Minneapolis, Minnesota. People have always told me to experience God's love, to let Him fill me with His love. Sunday He just poured it into me and it is terrific. I do not have to depend on people but on Him. He is the greatest person there is.

Dale Klassen, Mt. Lake, Minnesota. When I came down here I had been trying to find happiness, peace and love for a long time. All my friends were trying to find the same thing. I did not know where it was. I tried drugs and it was not there. Finally, I went to this church in Marshall (Minn.). I noticed how much love they had and it made me think.

I had a chance to come down here to this campus fellowship meeting so I came. I saw how happy everybody was and I wanted that. I knew that was where it was. I always had a hard time when I tried to be a real Christian. I couldn't do it. I found that I had not really accepted Christ as my saviour so I did and got filled with the Holy Spirit. It is really beautiful.

Tim Taylor, Lubbock, Texas. The Lord has opened new things to me. I realize that I can depend on Him. The fact is that you are not always going to feel good, but you know that you can still trust in the Lord. And even when I do not feel like it, I am still supposed to obey Him. That is one thing I really got out of this conference, that we are supposed to obey the Lord no matter what.

Some charismatics understand that the enthusiasm of converts for experiencing the gifts can lead to an unbalanced understanding of the Spirit-filled life. Father Edward O'Connor, a major spokesman for Catholic Pentecostalism, contributes a sobering note on this subject.

The Purpose of the Charisms*

"Charismania" consists in attributing excessive importance to the charisms. It has two forms, of which the first is the

* From Edward D. O'Connor, *The Pentecostal Movement of the Catholic Church* (Notre Dame: Ave Maria Press, 1971), pp. 226-28.

mentality which regards the charismatic as the sole or principal criterion of spiritual excellence. Thus, there are people who in effect identify spiritual growth with a more abundant exercise of charisms. The persons they admire and aspire to imitate are those whose charisms are the most spectacular. They forget that love alone is the measure of Christian spirituality. They know nothing of that life which is "hidden with Christ in God" (Col. 3:3) through the humility and meekness learned from the Savior (Matt. 11:29).

The same people are prone to evaluate prayer meetings by the amount of charismatic activity that occurs in them. When there have been several prophecies and perhaps a healing, they think the prayer meeting was great; whereas when nothing but prayer occurs, even though it has been a very deep prayer, they are disappointed.

To counteract this misconception, it needs to be stressed constantly 1) that the charisms are not goals in themselves, and are not given simply to be enjoyed, but are intended to promote the growth of love; 2) that a single moment of deep prayer is worth infinitely more than the most spectacular miracle or amazing prophecy. For true prayer is actual union with God, and this is the goal to which the charisms are subservient. The charisms can be abused (Matt. 7:22), but prayer cannot;[1] 3) that there can be deep spiritual life in one who has no (preternatural) charisms, and spectacular charismatic works in one who is an enemy of Christ as was pointed out in the preceding chapter.

The second form of "charismania" consists in expecting charismatic activity to take the place of the natural exercise of the human faculties or the ordinary workings of Church office. Thus, there are people who want their entire lives

---

[1] It is, of course, possible to use prayer as a pretext for neglecting one's duties. But in such a case, the prayer is not genuine. It is only a semblance just as external as the charisms, and hypocritical besides. That is why in the text I speak of true prayer.

to be guided by heavenly messages and revelations, and hence neglect the planning and deliberation that are within their power. Some people want all sicknesses to be healed miraculously, and refuse to see a doctor or to take medicine. On similar grounds, others would like to see theological study and sermon preparation replaced by a kerygma of purely charismatic inspiration, and the institutional offices in the Church, of bishop, pastor and clergy, replaced by a purely charismatic leadership.

Christ, however, did not build his Church on the charisms. He built it, in the first place, out of human beings. The natural human faculties of mind, will and emotions, as well as the cultural and social achievements that proceed from them, are not meant to be displaced by supernatural powers, but are themselves to be integrated into the fullness of the Kingdom of God and the Body of Christ. After all, man's natural faculties are gifts of God just as truly as are the charisms.

Secondly, Christ built a church structured upon offices appointed by him, not determined by the charisms. Not one of the Twelve had manifested any charismatic powers before Christ gave them their apostolic mission. Similarly, when it became necessary to find a replacement for Judas, the apostles did not wait for a charismatic figure to emerge, but selected the man who seemed best qualified, and appointed him (Acts 1:15-26).[2]

But in this Church, composed of human beings, and given its structure by offices instituted by Christ, there also occur the charisms. These are free, unpredictable workings of the Spirit, that do not arise out of the natural resources of the

[2] The fact that they cast lots in selecting Matthias over Joseph Barsabas does not affect the issue here. The point is that the man was appointed to the office by those already in authority; he did not establish himself in a position of leadership by his charismatic or other gifts.

human psyche, nor from the authoritative initiatives of the hierarchy, but from the direct intervention of the living Lord who wishes to demonstrate that he is still sovereign over nature and over the Church.

There are, therefore, three distinct sources of energy and activity in the Christian life: natural, ecclesiastical and charismatic. The natural includes all that arises from human nature. The ecclesiastical includes all that arises from Christ's institution. The charismatic, finally, includes that which arises from the free inspiration of the Holy Spirit. Not one of these is meant to replace the others, but each has its own proper function.

Obviously many observers of the new Pentecostalism who are themselves witnessing Christians disagree with the doctrine of Holy Spirit Baptism. The following selection by a Professor of Systematic Theology at Calvin Theological Seminary, Grand Rapids, Michigan, and widely published author in this general field represents the most thoughtful and responsible criticism of this doctrine.

Is the Second Blessing Necessary?*

In the rest of this chapter let us see whether the New Testament outside of the Book of Acts supports Neo-Pentecostal teaching on Spirit-baptism.

There is perhaps no chapter in the New Testament which is as rich in teachings about the Holy Spirit as Romans 8. Here, after affirming that those who are "in the flesh" (that is, unregenerate) cannot please God, Paul goes on to say, "But ye are not in the flesh but in the Spirit, if so be that the Spirit of God dwelleth in you" (v. 9). The words "if so be" are not intended to suggest that certain Christians do

* Reprinted by permission from Anthony A. Hoekema, *Holy Spirit Baptism* (Grand Rapids: Wm. B. Eerdmans Publishing Co., 1972), pp. 26-29, 90-93.

not have the Spirit dwelling within them, for Paul states emphatically in the next sentence, "But if any man hath not the Spirit of Christ, he is none of his." You as regenerated persons, Paul is saying here to his Roman Christian readers, are no longer in the flesh but in the Spirit, and to be in the Spirit means that the Spirit is dwelling in you. To dwell means to reside permanently. To suggest, as our Neo-Pentecostal friends do, that the Spirit comes into one's life only in a small trickle when one is first converted and does not come in His totality until some later time contradicts the plain teaching of this verse. If you're a Christian, Paul says to us all, the Spirit is dwelling in you. What more can He do than to dwell? Can He double-dwell or triple-dwell?

To the same effect is I Corinthians 3:16, where Paul says to the entire Corinthian church, "Know ye not that ye are a temple of God, and that the Spirit of God dwelleth in you?" The point is made in somewhat different words in I Corinthians 6:19, "Or know ye not that your body is a temple of the Holy Spirit which is in you?" These words are spoken not just about certain believers in distinction from others but about all believers, since all believers have been "bought with a price" (v. 20). The apostolic benediction of II Corinthians 13:14 implies, further, that all believers may enjoy the continued presence and fellowship of the Holy Spirit: "The grace of the Lord Jesus Christ and the love of God and the fellowship of the Holy Spirit be with you all" (RSV).

In his letter to the Colossians Paul is combating the views of those who say that in order to attain to the "higher Christian life" a Christian needs something in addition to faith in Christ. The "something more" required included such things as circumcision, the keeping of the Jewish feast days, and a rigorous type of asceticism. Paul replies to this kind of false teaching in these words: "In him [Christ] dwelleth all the fulness of the Godhead bodily, and in him ye are made full" (2:9-10). Since you have already been made full in Christ, Paul is saying, you do not need to follow disciplines additional to faith in Christ in order to attain a greater fullness in Christ. If, now, the believer—as Paul here teaches—has been made full in Christ through faith, has he not also been made full in the Holy Spirit? Or is there a separation between the Persons of the Trinity? Can one have all of Christ but only part of the Holy Spirit? Does not Christ dwell in us by His Spirit (cf. Rom. 8:9 with v. 10)?

Nowhere in the New Testament, in fact, do we find believers asking for a baptism in the Spirit of the sort advocated by Neo-Pentecostals—a post-conversion experience in which they receive the total presence of a Spirit whom they had previously possessed only in part—and nowhere do we find the apostles instructing believers to seek such a baptism. Rather, we find Paul saying to the Galatians, "If we live by the Spirit, by the Spirit let us also walk" (Gal. 5:25). If we have been regenerated, Paul teaches here, we live by the Spirit, since only the Spirit can bring us from death to life. If this be so, then by that same Spirit in whom we live let us also walk. Paul does not say: Wait for a baptism with the Spirit so that you will be able to walk in Him. He says: Walk more fully in or by that Spirit whom you already have, in whom you already live!

To the same effect is Paul's teaching in Ephesians. In 1:13 he writes to the believers who are the recipients of this letter, "In whom [Christ] ye also having heard the word of the truth, the gospel of your salvation—in whom, having also believed, ye were sealed with the Holy Spirit of promise." All of you who are believers, Paul is saying, received the Holy Spirit when you believed, and have been sealed by that Spirit—given the assurance that all that God has promised His people is now yours. Later in the epistle, however, in 5:18, he writes, "And be not drunken with wine, wherein is riot, but be filled with the Spirit." The verb, "be filled," is the present tense in Greek, implying continuation. We could translate it as follows: "Be continually filled with the Spirit." The passage describes, not a momentary experience, but a lifelong challenge. So what Paul is saying to the Ephesians and to us is not this: After your conversion you must all seek a once-for-all experience in which you receive the total presence of a Spirit whom you previously possessed only in part. Rather, what he is saying is this: You must all daily and hourly yield yourselves completely to that Spirit who is already dwelling within you.

We must conclude, then, that the New Testament does not support Neo-Pentecostal teaching on Spirit-baptism. To insist that believers need to walk more fully by that Spirit in whom they already live, or to yield themselves more completely to that Spirit by whom they have already been sealed, is sound Scriptural teaching—teaching which the church today sorely needs. But to say that a Christian needs a "baptism in the Spirit" subsequent to his conversion, in which the Spirit now enters the believer's life in His totality, is to distort the clear teaching of Scripture and to confuse the minds of God's people.

(Note: from this point on the expressions "baptism in the Spirit" and "Spirit-baptism" will be in quotation marks whenever they are used in the Neo-Pentecostal sense, in distinction from what has been shown above to be the Biblical sense.

The New Testament clearly teaches that we must commit our lives to God decisively and permanently. In Romans 12:1, for example, Paul puts it this way: "I beseech you therefore, brethren, by the mercies of God, to present your bodies a living sacrifice, holy, acceptable to God, which is your spiritual service." The verb rendered present is in the aorist tense, suggesting a once-for-all commitment. This verb is sometimes used to describe the bringing of a sacrifice to the temple priest. Paul, using the imagery of the Old Testament sacrificial ritual, here appeals to his readers to offer their bodies to God as living sacrifices—that is, to present to God their total selves, in gratitude for God's infinite mercies. This offering is to be a once-for-all transaction; it is a decision which permanently determines the direction of one's life.

Ordinarily this once-for-all commitment should occur at the time of conversion, and for most Christians it undoubtedly does take place then. Yet it may very well happen that a person who thinks he was converted at an early age finds that he did not totally commit his life to God at that time, and therefore makes such a total commitment later in life. It would not be proper to call this a post-conversion experience, since the earlier experience was not a genuine conversion. Another possibility, however, is far more common: Christians who have been truly converted may find themselves undergoing periods of spiritual laxity, so that they feel a need for reaffirming their commitment to God or for yielding themselves anew to Him. Such experiences, however, would be reconfirmations or reaffirmations of decisions which had been made before. One would not be justified in calling such reaffirmations "baptisms in the Spirit," since, as we have seen, the Scriptures teach that all believers are baptized in the Spirit at the time of conversion.

It may very well be that what our Neo-Pentecostal brothers call "baptism in the Spirit" is either a first conversion of someone who had been only a nominal Christian before, or a renewed commitment to the Lord of someone who, though truly converted before, has now for some time been grieving the Spirit. While rejecting Neo-Pentecostal teachings on "Spirit-baptism" and tongue-speaking, we may well be happy and grateful for experiences of the sort just described. When unbelievers are brought into living fellowship with Christ and when believers are enabled to live richer and more fruitful Christian lives than they lived before, we can only thank God. The proof of this living fellowship with Christ, however, is not to be sought in spectacular or ecstatic phenomena, but in the growing presence of the fruit of the Spirit.

We may sum up as follows: Believers do not need to seek a post-conversion "baptism in the Spirit," but they do need to be continually filled with the Spirit who dwells within. Let us then enter into the fulness of our heritage as children of God. Let us experience the full richness of union with Christ. Let us see ourselves, not just as depraved sinners, but as new creatures in Christ. Let us grasp by faith the infinite resources we have in Christ. Let us daily be filled with the Spirit, and let our lives reflect the radiancy of that Spirit. May God grant us all increasingly to know the love of Christ which passes knowledge, and to be filled with all the fulness of God.

Study Guide Questions for Chapter 6

1. Do you think some of the confusion over this doctrine comes from the Pentecostalist use of the word "Baptism" for the second blessing?
2. If the Baptism in the Holy Spirit is not necessary for salvation, is it worth the enthusiasm and dedication the Pentecostalists give it?
3. How might this doctrine tend to divide a congregation? How might it unite a congregation?
4. What is the difference between this doctrine and that of conversion?

7. Speaking in Tongues

The most controversial gift of the Baptism in the Holy Spirit is the ability of the believer to speak in tongues (or practice "glossolalia"). To some critics it is a normal process of verbalizing deeply felt ideas, and should not be considered as the product of a disturbed person; see the exhaustive study by a sociolinguist, Professor William J. Samarin of the University of Toronto, Tongues of Men and Angels: The Religious Language of Pentecostalism. To others, such as Merrill F. Unger, an Old Testament scholar at Dallas Theological Seminary, tongues is unbiblical since the gift died out of usage in the apostolic era (see his New Testament Teaching on Tongues).*

To all those who have experienced the gift, however, and to many sympathetic nonglossolaliacs, such as Morton T. Kelsey and Father Kilian McDonnell, the phenomenon is unquestionably a supernatural gift from God through the Holy Spirit Baptism. Almost everyone in every school of thought on tongues today does agree on one thing: if the gift is made to be the requirement for participation in a local congregation or prayer meeting, then it no longer serves to build up the community. Further, all observers agree that whether of supernatural origins or not, the private meditational use of tongues contributes positively to personal edification and deeper spiritual life.

As the following selections will show, however, that is about the extent of agreement. The spokesmen presented here speak to the major issues of tongues, and represent the consensus of opinion for the position which they take.

This selection, by Don Basham, attempts to define the experience of speaking in tongues and to answer some of the major objections to it.

The Value of Speaking in Tongues*

Can I receive the baptism in the Holy Spirit without speaking in tongues?

* Don Basham, *A Handbook on Holy Spirit Baptism* ($1.00). Available from Whitaker Books, 504 Laurel Drive, Monroeville, Pa. 15146.

"With God all things are possible" (Matt. 19:26), therefore the answer to this question is yes. However, it is a qualified yes! I personally know two people who received the baptism in the Holy Spirit in English rather than with unknown tongues. Both were exceptionally sensitive, prophetic men, true spiritual giants of our time. One is Dr. Frank Laubach, through whom the Holy Spirit manifests Himself supernaturally in English. The other was Rufus Mosley who, some months after his baptism in the Holy Spirit, began to speak in tongues and continued to witness faithfully to their value until his death. In a booklet entitled, "How To Enter, Abide, and Increase in Union With Jesus Christ" he makes this excellent statement:

My feeling is that we must not be dogmatic and say that no one can have the baptism of the Holy Spirit unless he speaks in tongues. God, of course, can speak in English and in every tongue of men and angels. But He now seems a little more real to me when He speaks in tongues, especially if I am given the meaning of what is spoken. And when an ignorant person speaks in languages entirely unknown to him, it is easy to see that he is not doing the speaking.

The Lord will do wonders for us even if we are prejudiced against tongues, if we are willing to yield at other points. He uses well the all of us that is yielded to Him while he waits for all that is not yielded to be yielded. He doesn't cut us off because we are not yielded at every point, but I have an idea that those of us who have been prejudiced against tongues will be faced around and will like them best of all (p. 41).

So we must admit that the baptism in the Holy Spirit can be received without the manifestation of tongues, but we encourage no one to seek the baptism without expecting tongues. Both our understanding of spiritual gifts and our willingness to receive them affect what gifts and manifestations will appear. SOMETHING IS MISSING IN YOUR SPIRITUAL LIFE IF YOU HAVE RECEIVED THE HOLY SPIRIT YET HAVE NOT SPOKEN IN TONGUES. Those Spirit-filled Christians who have not yet spoken in tongues will receive a precious added assurance of God's presence and power when they do.

True, speaking in tongues is controversial, but if we are really seeking all God wants to bestow we must seek God's blessings on God's terms, not ours. It is better to hold to the scriptural pattern than be swayed by human prejudices. All who speak in tongues have the authority of scripture behind their experience. They do not need to defend their baptism in the Holy Spirit by saying, "Yes, I have received the baptism . . . BUT . . . I do not speak in tongues." So if you tell me you have received the Holy Spirit without speaking in tongues, I do not deny your claim. But when you witness to me that you do speak in tongues I rejoice because your experience is fully consistent with scripture.

We encourage everyone seeking to be filled with the Holy Spirit to seek the baptism on scriptural terms, fully expecting to speak in tongues when they receive.

Those who ask the question, "Do I have to speak in tongues?" make it sound as if they are being asked to swallow an unpleasant dose of medicine. Their question indicates they believe tongues something to be endured rather than enjoyed! Speaking in tongues is a blessed experience! It is a joy and a privilege to be able to communicate with the Lord in this new and exciting manner. Someone has rightly said, "You don't have to speak in tongues, you get to!" Or, as Dr. David du Plessis comments, "You don't have to, but you will."

Any person receiving the baptism in the Holy Spirit can, from the moment he accepts the Holy Spirit into his life in this new and powerful way, speak in tongues. The actual physical process is discussed elsewhere in this book. But rest assured that anyone filled with the Holy Spirit can speak in tongues.

Sometimes one receiving the baptism may refuse—because of shyness or fear or false teaching—to yield his tongue and lips at the moment he receives the Spirit, and so is robbed of this blessing for days or even weeks. But time and again we have heard the testimony of such persons upon eventually yielding and receiving tongues. They admit that had they not resisted or backed away, they would have spoken in tongues the moment they received the baptism in the Holy Spirit.

What is "speaking in tongues"?

Speaking or praying in tongues is a form of prayer in which the Christian yields himself to the Holy Spirit and receives from the Spirit a supernatural language with which to praise God. It is a miraculous manifestation of God's power, but one which combines both human and divine elements and which expresses both human and divine initiative. It is truly a co-operation between the Christian and the Holy Spirit.

Many people misunderstand what takes place when they hear someone praying or speaking in tongues. They are apprehensive over what might happen to them if they "let themselves go like that" or let "some other power take over." They assume the person is completely passive and that the Holy Spirit is doing it all. This is a completely erroneous impression of what is taking place. The person himself is very actively participating in the experience. As someone bluntly put it, "Without the Holy Spirit you can't, but without you the Holy Spirit won't."

Stated in the simplest way: Man does the speaking while the Holy Spirit furnishes the words. Acts 2:4 says, "They were all filled with the Holy Spirit and began to speak in other tongues as the Spirit gave them utterance." A free translation might read, ". . . they . . . began to speak as the Spirit gave them words to say."

Speaking in tongues is a way of praying which liberates the spirit within and strengthens the Christian in a wonderful manner. The primary purpose of it is for use in one's own devotional life. Careful restrictions are placed upon its public use. (See 1st Cor. 14:18-19, 27-28.)

Don't the Scriptures, "Do all speak with tongues?" 1st Cor. 12:30) and "If any speak in tongues, let there be only two or at most three . . ." (1st Cor. 14:27) indicate that not all Christians are meant to speak in tongues?

Certainly this has been used as an extensive argument by those who oppose speaking in tongues. In fact, many use Paul's statement, "let only two or three speak," not to limit tongues but to prohibit them entirely. Both these Scriptures must be considered in any discussion of tongues, but only in connection with Paul's statement in 1st Cor. 14:5: "Now I want you all to speak in tongues . . ." How do we reconcile, "let there be only two or at most three . . ." and "I want you all to speak . . ."? Is Paul contradicting himself? No.

The confusion is cleared away when we consider the two sets of circumstances in which speaking in tongues appear in the New Testament. They appear both as a sign and as a gift. They appear as a sign or outward evidence which accompanies the baptism in the Holy Spirit in Acts 2:4, Acts 10:45, Acts 19:6 and Mark 16:17. They appear as a gift in Paul's references in 1st Corinthians 12 and 14.

Now in Acts, where tongues appear as a sign, all who received the baptism in the Holy Spirit spoke in tongues. No limitation or restriction is placed on the manifestation nor is there any suggestion that some received tongues while others did not. Nor is there any attempt to teach or instruct the recipients in the "proper use" of tongues. Speaking in tongues came to all, serving as the sign or evidence of the Holy Spirit's arrival in power upon them. I believe it is safe and correct to say that there is no such thing as misuse of tongues when they initially appear, at the time of one's receiving the baptism in the Holy Spirit.

But in 1st Cor. chapters 12-14, we find Paul discussing speaking in tongues as a gift among other gifts, to be used in the services of the church, only as the Holy Spirit directs, for "the common good" (1st Cor. 12:7). Here Paul treats speaking in tongues, not in terms of receiving, but in terms of exercising the ability at a given time in the service of worship. He was explaining to those who had received the sign tongue when they were baptized in the Holy Spirit, and who could now manifest this ability to praise God in other languages, how, in church, any manifestation of tongues should fall in the same category as other manifestations of the Spirit such as prophecy, the word of wisdom, etc. Paul makes it clear that in church, if some individual is moved by the Holy Spirit to manifest tongues, it should be accompanied by the gift of interpretation so that the whole worshipping assembly may benefit by it (1st Cor. 14:27). Yet, even here, Paul qualifies his statement by adding that prayer in tongues without interpretation, i.e., the sign tongue, may also be exercised during the church service, but only silently, so as not to disturb or disrupt the public worship service (1st Cor. 14:28).

Certainly in regard to speaking in tongues aloud, in church, with the gift of interpretation to follow, the question, "Do all speak with tongues?" must be answered with an emphatic No!

However, when we encourage those seeking the baptism in the Holy Spirit to seek it in terms of the initial scriptural evidence of speaking in tongues we do not assume that all receiving tongues will be led by the Spirit to manifest the gift in a public worship service. Experience indicates that only a small percentage of those who manifest speaking in tongues at the time they receive the baptism in the Holy Spirit will ever be used for a public manifestation of tongues and interpretation in church. By far the most common use of tongues is during one's own private prayer time.

Essentially, what we have said here is, the accounts in the book of Acts show how the baptism in the Holy Spirit with speaking in tongues is received, while Paul's instructions in 1st Corinthians show how speaking in tongues is to be properly used and controlled in services of the church.

Why should I speak in tongues?

The most obvious answer to this question is that the Scriptures encourage it. Jesus said it was one of the signs which was to follow the ministry of Christians; "And these signs will accompany those who believe . . . they will speak with new tongues . . ." (Mk. 16:17). And Paul, while recognizing the need for propriety in the public manifestation of tongues, nevertheless urges Christians to receive and make use of this significant gift. "Earnestly desire spiritual gifts . . . Now I want you all to speak in tongues . . . I thank God I speak in tongues more than you all . . ." (1st Cor. 14:1, 5, 18). As the late Rev. Samuel Shoemaker observed, "The Christian needs every gift God offers."

The willingness to yield our tongues to God may also indicate a more profound surrender than almost any other act. The tongue is the primary instrument of expression of the human personality, and until God has dominion over the tongue, His control over us is relatively slight.

So the tongue is a little member and boasts of great things. How great a forest is set ablaze by a small fire. And the tongue is a fire. The tongue is an unrighteous world among our members, staining the whole body, setting on fire the cycle of nature and set on fire by hell.

For every kind of beast and bird, of reptile and sea creature can be tamed and has been tamed by humankind, but no human can tame the tongue—a restless evil, full of deadly poison—James 3:5-8.

In addition, experience shows that prayer in tongues, which the Scriptures also refer to as "prayer in the Spirit" (see 1st Cor. 14:14-15, Eph. 6:18) enables us to pray with an ability and authority not our own. We do not always know how to pray in a given situation, but, holding the need up to the Father we pray in tongues, knowing that our prayers are guided by the Holy Spirit.

When we cry, "Abba, Father," it is the Spirit Himself bearing witness with our spirit that we are children of God. . . . Likewise the Spirit helps us in our weakness, for we do not know how to pray as we ought, but the Spirit Himself intercedes for us with sighs too deep for words. And He who searches the hearts of men knows what the mind of the Spirit is, because the Spirit intercedes for the saints according to the will of God—Rom. 8:15-16, 26-27.

Why speak in tongues? Because it grants the Christian a freedom in prayer which enables him to praise God extravagantly, beyond the limiting confines of known speech. Our Lord had nothing but praise for those who worshipped Him extravagantly, or served or trusted him extravagantly; the poor widow who gave God all the money she had (Luke 21:1-4), the Roman centurion and his extravagant faith in Jesus' healing power (Matt. 8:5-13) and Mary, who was extravagant in her devotion in anointing Him with precious ointment (Matt. 26:6-13). Yet many of us are so niggardly and pinched in our relationship with God that any real freedom in prayer or worship is beyond us. Such freedom can come through praying in tongues.

It may help also to realize there are strong Biblical reasons for speaking in tongues. Dr. Henry Ness, in his booklet,

"The Baptism with The Holy Spirit" lists twenty Bible reasons for speaking in tongues.

1. Speaking with tongues as the Holy Spirit gives the utterance is the unique spiritual gift identified with the Church of Jesus Christ. Prior to the day of Pentecost, all other gifts, miracles, and spiritual manifestations had been in evidence during the Old Testament times. On the Day of Pentecost, this new phenomenon came into evidence and became uniquely identified with the Church (Acts 2:4) and 1st Corinthians, chapters 12-14.

2. Speaking with tongues was ordained by God for the Church (1st Cor. 12:28, 14:21).

3. Speaking with tongues is a specific fulfillment of prophecy (Isaiah 28:11; 1st Cor. 14:21; Joel 2:28; Acts 2:16).

4. Speaking with tongues is a sign OF the believer (Jn. 7:38, 39, Mk. 16:17).

5. Speaking with tongues is a sign TO the unbeliever (1st Cor. 14:22).

6. Speaking with tongues is a proof of the resurrection and glorification of Jesus Christ (Jn. 16:7, Acts 2:22, 25, 32, 33).

7. Speaking with tongues is an evidence of the baptism with the Holy Spirit (Jn. 15:26, Acts 2:4, 10:45, 46, 19:6).

8. Speaking with tongues is a means of preaching to men of other languages (Acts 2:6-11).

9. Speaking with tongues is a spiritual gift for self-edification (1st Cor. 14:4).

10. Speaking with tongues is a spiritual gift for spiritual edification for the Church (1st Cor. 14:5).

11. Speaking with tongues is a spiritual gift for communication with God in private worship (1st Cor. 14:2).

12. Speaking with tongues is a means by which the Holy

Spirit intercedes through us in prayer (Rom. 8:26, 1st Cor. 14:14).

13. Speaking with tongues is a spiritual gift for "singing in the Spirit" (Eph. 5:18-19, 1st Cor. 14:15).
14. The Apostle Paul was thankful to God for the privilege of speaking in tongues (1st Cor. 14:13).
15. The Apostle Paul desired that all would speak with tongues (1st Cor. 14:5).
16. Speaking with tongues is one of the gifts of the Spirit (1st Cor. 12:10).
17. The Apostle Paul ordered that speaking with tongues should not be forbidden (1st Cor. 14:39).
18. Isaiah prophetically refers to speaking with tongues as a "rest" (Isaiah 28:12, 1st Cor. 14:21).
19. Isaiah prophetically refers to speaking with tongues as a "refreshing" (Isaiah 28:12, 1st Cor. 14:21).
20. Speaking with tongues follows as a confirmation of the word of God when it is preached (Mk. 16:17, 20).

Why hasn't the gift of tongues been mentioned in the great revivals of the past?

The gift of tongues has been prominent in some great revivals of the past; barely mentioned in some, and ignored or disparaged in others. In the great Pentecostal outpouring which began in the first decade of this century, speaking in tongues was the most talked-about and controversial feature in the revival. This revival, which caught fire in the famed Azusa Street Mission in Los Angeles in 1906, gave birth to a number of the strong Pentecostal denominations in our country today.

But there is real spiritual truth in the statement; "What we receive from God is determined by what we expect from Him." In many an earlier revival though there were great manifestations of God's power, few people expected speaking in tongues to appear and few people saw them. Still, there are accounts of the revivals of John Wesley, Dwight Moody, Charles Finney and others which take note of speaking in tongues, although they never played a prominent part.

The Encyclopaedia Britannica states that speaking in tongues has recurred in Christian revivals of every age. There is also evidence in the reports of some revivals that where speaking in tongues appeared they were squelched as emotionalism even though shouting, laughing, crying, dancing and trembling, even rolling on the floor, were considered "genuine" signs of the Holy Spirit's working. It also seems apparent that speaking in tongues was in evidence in other revivals where singing and laughing in the Spirit were heard, but that the speaking in tongues simply passed unrecognized.

The significant portion here is Christenson's explanation that an utterance in tongues does not go through the mind but flows directly to God through Spirit-prompted prayer. This is a forthright explanation of a very controversial element within tongues-speaking.

Bypassing the Mind*

One immediately wonders, "What possible value can speaking in tongues have, if I have no idea what I am saying?" According to the Bible, even though you do not understand what you are saying, your spirit is in a state of prayer (I Cor. 14:14). But it is a praying with the spirit rather than the mind. It is neither an emotional nor intellectual act (although both emotion and intellect may be affected), but an act of spiritual worship.

* Reprinted by permission from *Speaking in Tongues*, by Larry Christenson, published and copyright 1968, Bethany Fellowship, Inc., Minneapolis, Minnesota 55438.

It would seem that prayer in which the mind is unfruitful would have little value. What blessing can it be to pray when you have no idea what you are praying about? Actually, this is one of its greatest blessings—the fact that it is not subject to the limitations of your human intellect. The human mind, wonderful as it is from the hand of the Creator, has limited knowledge, limited linguistic ability, limited understanding, and furthermore is inhibited with all manner of prejudice, little and large. Speaking in tongues is a God-appointed manner of praying which can bypass the limitations of the intellect. One may picture the difference something like this: A prayer with the mind comes upward from the heart, and must then pass through a maize of linguistic, theological, rational, emotional, and personal check-points before it is released upward. By the time it "gets out," it may be little more than a slender trickle. An utterance in tongues comes upward from the depths, but instead of being channeled through the mind, it bypasses the mind and flows directly to God in a stream of Spirit-prompted prayer, praise, and thanksgiving.

The author, a minister and former President of the Southern Baptist Convention, presents a penetrating critique from a strongly conservative position. Criticisms from the standpoint of a theological-psychological perspective are listed in the bibliography in John P. Kildahl's The Psychology of Speaking in Tongues, *included in this handbook's bibliography.*

Facts Concerning Modern Glossolalia*

Since Paul wrote his interpretation of speaking in tongues, almost two thousand years have passed. In reviewing that long history and in observing the phenomenon of modern-

---

* Taken from *The Holy Spirit in Today's World* by W. A. Criswell, copyright © 1966, by Zondervan Publishing House and used by permission.

day glossolalia, I have a definite interpretation that comes from the depth of my own soul. These observations will be made in factual presentations. "Just the facts, Mister. Just give us the facts." There are five of these plain, clearly recognized facts to be seen in ecclesiastical chronology and in contemporary Christendom.

First fact. The basic doctrine that lies back of glossolalian practice is wrong. That doctrine is this: that speaking in tongues is the necessary evidence of the filling (they use the word "baptism") of the Holy Spirit. This doctrine is in direct opposition to the distinct and emphasized teaching of the Word of God. In I Corinthians 12:13 Paul says that all the Christians at Corinth had been baptized by the Holy Spirit, had been added to the body of Christ. But in I Corinthians 12:28-30 Paul avows that all do not speak with tongues. If you have been saved, you have been made a member by Spirit baptism of the precious body of our Lord. "By one Spirit are we all baptized into one body" (I Corinthians 12:13). But whether you speak with tongues or not has nothing to do with the holy, heavenly baptism. The two are in nowise connected; neither is one the evidence of the other.

Again in Ephesians 5:18 we are emphatically enjoined to be filled with the Spirit. It is God's will that all be filled with the Spirit. But here, also, it must be observed in contradistinction to this injunction that we all be filled with the Spirit. The Apostle writes that we are not all given the gift of tongues. "Are all apostles? [No.] Are all prophets? [No.] Are all workers of miracles? [No.] Have all the gifts of healing? [No.] Do all speak with tongues? [No.]" (I Corinthians 12:29, 30). There is no such Scriptural teaching as that speaking in tongues is the sign of the filling ("baptism") of the Holy Spirit. It is a man-made doctrine and does not come from the Bible.

Second fact. In the years of my reading through Christian

history and of my studying the lives of great men of God, I have never once found an instance where a mighty hero of the faith spoke in unknown tongues. Preachers, missionaries, theologians, pioneers, translators, evangelists, all have come under review, but glossolalia is never a part of their lives. John Wesley will describe his Aldersgate experience, but never will he approach such a thing as speaking in tongues. Charles G. Finney will write in his famous *Autobiography* the fillings of the Holy Spirit that came in waves over his soul, but never will he intimate that he spoke in tongues. Dwight L. Moody will describe his marvelous infilling of love that swept his very being, but never does he suggest that he spoke in tongues. R. A. Torrey will write in a book on the baptism of the Holy Spirit, but his words of experience are pointedly directed against glossolalia. There is no exception to this witness, whether the great man of God live in the ancient or the medieval or the modern world. John Chrysostom (John the Golden-mouth), possibly the most eloquent preacher of all time and one of the most gifted commentators on the Scriptures, born in A.D. 345, pastor of the churches at Antioch and Constantinople, expressed even in his day puzzlement at Paul's account of the tongue-speaking situation at Corinth. He said: "The whole passage (I Corinthians 14:1-40) is exceedingly obscure and the obscurity is occasioned by our ignorance of the facts and the cessation of happenings which were common in those days but unexampled in our own." Glossolalia is always outside the circle of the life and experience of the great men of God who lived in Christian history.

Third fact. In the long story of the Church, after the days of the apostles, wherever the phenomenon of glossolalia has appeared it has been looked upon as heresy. Glossolalia mostly has been confined to the nineteenth and twentieth centuries. But wherever and however its appearance, it has never been accepted by the historical churches of Christendom. It has been universally repudiated by these churches as a doctrinal and emotional aberration.

The Amazing Way We Are Supposed to Receive the Baptism of the Holy Ghost

Fourth fact. Modern glossolalia is a bewildering development. In the last century (after a silence in tongue-speaking for hundreds of years) there appeared in England a man by the name of Edward Irving who presented himself as a prophet of God. He dressed like one (with long, uncut hair) and he looked like one (with a towering stature). He and his "Irvingites" began the tongue-speaking movement that has reached down to us today. Of him, rugged old Thomas Carlyle said, "God is evidently working miracles by hysterics."

The program of the glossolaliasts to teach us how to speak in tongues is something new for the books. A few days ago I received through the mail a tract concerning how to receive the "baptism" of the Holy Ghost and how to speak in unknown tongues. I quote from the tract: "How can I receive the Holy Ghost? All you have to do to be saved is to raise your hands up toward Heaven and turn your head up toward Heaven and begin praising God just as fast as you can and let your tongue go and let the Holy Ghost come in. Thousands of people receive the Holy Ghost this way. You can receive it too, if you will just let the Holy Ghost speak through your tongue." A book that I read, from a famous glossolaliast, gave specific instructions how anyone could receive the "baptism" of the Holy Ghost. "Raise up your hands and your eyes to heaven," he said, "and begin speaking words, sounds, syllables, and keep it up, faster, faster, faster, louder, louder words, more words, faster, faster, and it has happened! You have received the baptism of the Holy Ghost!" Seekers after the "baptism" are encouraged to remain in "tarrying meetings" in which they are taught to loosen the tongue by imitation of the leader in saying "ah-bah, ah-bah, beta, beta," etc. The leader will shake the lower jaw of a seeker to loosen it so that the gift will come. What am I to think about all of this? Is the Holy Third Person of the Trinity, the moving, mighty Spirit of God, thus controlled and directed by the loosening of the joints of the jaw? By the gibberish of senseless sounds? I am bewildered by the suggestion.

Fifth fact. As far as I have been able to learn, no real language is ever spoken by the glossolaliast. He truly speaks in an unknown and unknowable tongue. Tape recordings of those speaking in unknown tongues were played before the Toronto Institute of Linguistics. After these learned men in the science of phonetics had studied the recordings, they said, "This is no human language." At another time, other tape recordings were played before a group of governmental linguists at our nation's capitol. These gifted men found the sounds unrecognizable. "What they speak is meaningless to the human ear," was their verdict.

Sixth fact. Wherever and whenever glossolalia appears, it is always hurtful and divisive. There is no exception to this. It is but another instrument for the tragic torture of the body of Christ. I have seen some of our finest churches torn apart by the practice. I have seen some of our churches that were lighthouses for Christ in a pioneer and pagan land destroyed by the doctrine. In a revival situation that promised many souls for Jesus and a true outpouring of the Holy Spirit, the leader decimated it all by beginning to speak in tongues. He came to see me in Dallas. I said to him: "Had you driven these many miles to come and see me to say, 'I have been filled with the Holy Spirit, I have been led of the Lord to give to the work of the Kingdom ninety per cent of all I make and to live on the remaining ten per cent,' I would have said, 'Praise God, Hallelujah!' Had you driven all the way to Dallas to say to me, 'I have been filled with the Holy Spirit, I have resolved to pray six hours every day,' I would have said, 'Glory to God for such a commitment!' Had you come these many miles to my study to say to me, 'I have the visitation from heaven in my soul; I will win at least one person to Jesus every day,' I would have said, 'Bless the name of God for so meaningful a dedication!' But when you come over these many miles to see me and you say, 'I have received the baptism of the Holy Ghost, I am speaking in tongues,' I reply, 'Oh, oh, oh! What a tragedy! The work of the revival is ruined.'" And it was. No revival came. Only trouble, disorder, and confusion, as at Corinth.

I close with the avowal of the Apostle Paul: "Yet in the church I had rather speak five words with my understanding, that by my voice I might teach others also, then ten thousand words in an unknown tongue" (I Corinthians 14: 19).

The author is Executive Director, Institute for Ecumenical and Cultural Research, Collegeville, Minnesota, associated with St. John's University there. He is one of the most knowledgeable scholars in both classical and new Pentecostalism, although he is not himself a member of the charismatic movement. In this selection he attempts to achieve a balanced estimate of tongues rather than focusing only on a few elements in the movement.

The Theology of Speaking in Tongues*

From a theological point of view it is irrelevant whether tongues are a true language or not.[1] Classical Pentecostals

* Kilian McDonnell, *Catholic Pentecostalism: Problems in Evaluation* (Pecos, N.M.: Dove Publications, 1971), pp. 18-22.

[1] Bittlinger, *Glossolalia*, 24. For tongues outside of the New Testament cf. Stuart D. Currie, "Speaking in Tongues: Early Evidence Outside the New Testament," *Interpretation*, vol. 19 (1965), 274-294. Carlyle May, "A Survey of Glossolalia and Related Phenomena in Non-Christian Religions," *American Anthropologist*, vol. 58 (1965), 75-95.

would insist that tongues are a true language and most neo-Pentecostals, Protestant and Catholic, usually agree.[2] All Pentecostal literature, classical, Protestant and Catholic neo-Pentecostal, give examples of foreign languages which were spoken in the presence of someone competent in that language who verified the linguistic authenticity of what was spoken. However, when one accepts the Pentecostal presuppositions, namely that the language can be any language ever spoken, even languages no longer spoken, or even the language of the Angels (they cite 1 Cor. 13:1), the problems of scientific verification become staggering.[3] Also the kind of controlled situation necessary for a truly scientific study rarely obtains when a language is recognized in a Pentecostal meeting. Without this kind of controlled situation most scientists would not accept tongues as true languages, and would rather contend that the recognition of the language by someone linguistically competent is based

[2] D. G. Lillie, *Tongues Under Fire*, Fountain Trust, London, 1966, 38; Christenson, 22-27; Bloch-Hoell, 87. Though Bittlinger thinks that most of the cases of speaking in tongues are questions of a specialized language (*Kunstsprache*), he lists cases where it was claimed that the language was identified, *Glossolalia*, 24-26. Bittlinger, *ibid.*, 11 and passim considers speaking in tongues a natural phenomenon which becomes a charism when it is a function of the Kingdom: "Wie alle Charismen ist auch das Charisma des Sprachenredens ein natürliches Phanomen." This is much the same as Ernst Käsemann's conception of a charism. Cf. "Ministry and Community in the New Testament," *Essays on New Testament Themes*, SCM Press, London, 1964, 68-72, 78, 82. Ranaghan leaves open the question as to the linguisticality of tongues, *Catholic Pentecostals*, 194. Ford seems to consider tongues a pure language, *Jubilee*, 16, 16. For a purely linguistic analysis cf. William J. Samarin, "The Linguisticality of Glossolalia," *The Hartford Quarterly*, vol. 8 (1968), 49-75; Samarin, "Glossolalia as Learned Behaviour," *Canadian Journal of Theology*, vol. 15 (January, 1969), 60-64.

[3] Christenson, *Speaking in Tongues*, 23, 24 tells of the German linguist, Prof. Eugene Rapp, who, it is claimed, speaks 45 languages. Rapp contends, "I would need at least sixteen pages of phonetically transcribed script to study and analyze before I could make a certain judgment (whether what was spoken is a true language)."

on psychological rather than linguistic factors. From an exegetical point of view it does not seem possible to decide the question.[4]

While most Catholic Pentecostals would consider the gift of tongues a gift of a true language, they would show a little impatience with the outsider's preoccupation with what the Pentecostals consider the most peripheral aspects of the problem. For them the issue is not tongues, but the fullness of life in the Spirit. The gift of tongues is a manifestation of this fullness and is only one of a number of possible manifestations. They would also concede that it is the lowest of the gifts. Catholic Pentecostals, as others in the movement, are more concerned with tongues as a gift of prayer.[5] In fieldwork the researcher frequently hears Catholic Pentecostals tell of a new depth in their prayer lives. They find themselves, they say, praying at a deeper level than they have prayed before, and they are greatly drawn to prayer. Their prayer has a marked trinitarian character to a degree not found in most Catholic groups. Perhaps the most significant aspect of their prayer life is the dominance of the prayer of praise. For many of them this concern for praise is the revelation of a new dimension. They had often recited the "Glory to God in the highest" of the Mass but had never really thought of praise as the basic orientation of their life of prayer. It is the role of praise in their prayer

[4] Whether glossolalia is a true language or not has been discussed at length by biblical scholars. Cf. "Langues (Don des)," *Dictionaire de la Bible*, Letouzey et Ané, Paris, 1908; "Glossolalie," *Bibel-Lexikon*, Benzinger, Einsiedeln, 1951; "Zungenrede," *Die Religion in Geschichte und Gegenwart*, 3rd ed., 1962; Frank W. Beare, "Speaking with *The Journal of Biblical Literature*, vol. 83 (1964), 229-46.

[5] Killian, *The Priest*, 25, 611-613. Killian says that speaking in tongues "is not unlike infused contemplation. In both types of prayer the mind is unfruitful." Killian thinks that tongues have a greater social value than contemplation and are well adapted to the contemporary activist mentality. Cf. also O'Connor, *Ave Maria*, 105, 8; Ford, *Jubilee*, 16, 13.

life that makes their prayer attitudes essentially those of joy and peace.[6]

The most characteristic activity of all Pentecostals is prayer, so much so that a casual observer would be led to think that it was simply a prayer movement. Undoubtedly it is this aspect of the movement which attracts many who get involved. They find that their prayer needs are not being met in the institutional churches. This does not mean that they desire to separate themselves from the structures of the church. Rather they find a need to supplement the more formal parish worship with a more informal, more directly experimental form of worship.

Part of the vocabulary which Catholic Pentecostalism has taken over from classical Pentecostalism is the talk of a hunger for God. This is more than just a verbal borrowing as Catholic Pentecostals, like classical and neo-Pentecostals, have a deep love of prayer which corresponds in the worship dimension to this hunger for God.

Though much of the theology is pneumatological in orientation, Christ is at the center of their religious consciousness. Speaking of the Notre Dame experience Ranaghan relates: "As each of us learned of what the other was doing, we rejoiced to see that in each case our testimony was not about tongues; not even primarily about the Holy Spirit. But wherever we went our talk was about Jesus Christ and the power of His saving love to transform men and man's world." [7]

Catholic Pentecostals sometimes raise the suspicions of other Catholics that their talk about baptism in the Holy Spirit, fullness of life in the Holy Spirit and exercise of the gifts is, as a matter of fact, a species of instant contempla-

---

[6] Ranaghan, *Catholic Pentecostals*, 52, 70, 85, 103 106; Ford, *Jubilee*, 16, 17; O'Connor, *Ave Maria*, 105, 9; Wullenweber, *St. Anthony Messenger*, 76, 21.

[7] *Acts*, 1, 28.

tion. Early in the tradition of classical Pentecostalism it was recognized that baptism in the Holy Spirit and the exercise of the gifts is not an indication of spiritual maturity. Indeed, there is a general recognition among all Pentecostals that he who exercises a gift of the Spirit is not by any necessity more mature spiritually than he who possesses no obvious gift. [8] For this reason all Pentecostals like to emphasize the "body function" of the gifts, that is, gifts are directed to the building up of the body of Christ (I Cor. 12: 27), and are subject to judgment of the body of Christ (I Cor. 12:29).

Among the more puzzling features to observers about Holy Spirit Baptism and tongues is that leaders in the more theologically conservative bodies are more critical of these than spokesmen from the more liberal traditions. A brief but pointed example of this is the following selection, written by the Dean of the Graduate Seminary, Phillips University, a part of the Christian Church (Disciples of Christ).

Nothing More than a Noisy Gong? *

[Editor's Note: After a brief review of the biblical teachings on tongues in 1 Corinthians, the author draws these conclusions.] Jealousy and rivalry over the practice of tongues is childish (1 Cor. 14:20). "I can do something that you can't . . . I have something that you don't." Gnosticism met the same danger, "I know something that you don't." Most

[8] "The Baptism in the Spirit does *not* make a believer sinlessly perfect, and the New Testament does *not* make spiritual gifts a sign of holiness." Gee, *Concerning Spiritual Gifts,* 70; cf. also Gee, "Do 'Tongues' Matter?" *Pentecost,* No. 45 (September, 1958), 17; Bittlinger, representing a neo-Pentecostal tradition, contends that "the possession of spiritual gifts is . . . in no sense a measure of Christian maturity." *Gifts and Graces,* 25. Ranaghan, *Catholic Pentecostals,* 182.

* From J. Daniel Joyce, " 'Do All Speak with Tongues?'—No! Do Any Speak with Tongues?—Maybe," *The Christian,* May 30, 1971, pp. 678-79.

of the disturbance now caused by the practice of tongues has its roots in this kind of understanding and rivalry.

The modern-day manifestations of tongues are characterized by inarticulate sounds and imperfect utterances. They are sounds that simulate words, a sort of pseudo-language. There is much alliteration and repetition, many nonsense syllables, such as are used by children, and many coined words. If a foriegn language is involved, and I don't believe it is, it is scraps of that language picked up by the speaker here and there. Every case that has been scientifically investigated, as far as I know, is explicable by recognized psychological laws.

One of the dangers in all of this is that Christian experience will be seen as Christian only when extraordinary deeds and manifestations of the Spirit are present. The craving for these manifestations eventuated in the apocryphal Acts of the Apostles. Our religious experience, as that of Paul, is wonderful, but it can never be made normative for another. If one speaks just to convince himself that he has it, not understanding what he is saying, he simply speaks into the air (1 Cor. 14:9). Everyone must accept responsibility for his experience in these regards. If he tears up a church with this highly individualized expcrience, he must accept full responsibility before God for that destruction. Each one must walk in love and submit to the other for Christ's sake. Only where this mutual subordination exists, and the church in turn subordinates itself to Christ, can the Holy Spirit fill the church and manifest the unity of the church.

But spirit-endowed men become arrogant, and this gift puffs up, just as knowledge puffs up. This lessens the concept of the Church as a community of the Spirit. Divine and demonic ecstasy are at times indistinguishable (1 Cor. 12:2). Ecstasy is not unambiguous, which means that it cannot be used to verify the presence of the Holy Spirit.

Love is the evidence of the possession of the Spirit, and the fruits of the Spirit are clearly set forth.

The legitimate heir of this gift of glossolalia is the gift of the Spirit to the Church, which makes the saving work of Christ present for the hearer and worshipper. It takes the word of the preacher and teacher and speaks to all kinds of needs, some entirely unknown to the speaker himself. The essence of the existence of the Church is life in the Spirit. The kingdom of God does not consist in talk or in words, but in demonstrations of the Spirit. We live by the Spirit and walk by the Spirit (Galatians 5:25). It is impossible for the legitimate heir of this gift to cause trouble in the church today, because "If I speak in the tongues of men and angels, but have not love, I am a noisy gong or a clanging cymbal" (1 Corinthians 13:1). Therefore, whoever is tearing up the unity of the Church in any place, or giving the impression of insanity, or edifying himself at the expense of the Church, or creating jealousy and rivalry, or speaking unintelligible or uninterpreted words, is nothing more than a noisy gong.

Study Guide Questions for Chapter 7

1. Do you think speaking in tongues is a scripturally proven sign of having received a gift through the Baptism in the Holy Spirit?
2. Do you find merit in the new Pentecostal argument that although the speaker in tongues may not know in English what he is saying, he is nonetheless undergoing an authentic religious experience?
3. What dangers are there to be found in Christenson's position that speaking in tongues is in actuality an experience which bypasses the mind?

8. The Gift of Healing

No less spectacular a gift than tongues is the Pentecostal gift of healing physical and mental ailments. Although the participants do not agree on every phase of this charism, almost all of them would accept the pro-healing arguments presented in this chapter. They would also accept the explanation that much of mankind's illness and trouble is caused by Satan and his demons who must be driven from a potential believer before the Baptism in the Holy Spirit can be received. The selections in this chapter attempt to present a representative cross section of new Pentecostal beliefs on healing and demons. See also the recently published exhaustive study, Morton T. Kelsey's Healing and Christianity in Ancient Thought and Modern Times.

The mass healing rally is one of the most popular means of spreading Pentecostal teachings. One such meeting is described here by the religion editor of the Minneapolis Star, Willmar Thorkelson. *Of special interest is the enthusiastic welcome given Miss Kuhlman in Minneapolis–St. Paul, long regarded respectively as bastions of conservative Scandinavian Lutheranism and Irish Catholicism.*

Twenty Thousand Flock to Faith Healer*

An estimated 20,000 persons yesterday jammed the Minneapolis Auditorium in hopes of witnessing the psychic healing ministry of a woman evangelist, Kathryn Kuhlman.

About 14,000 of them got into the auditorium's arena, while thousands more stood in auditorium halls for more than three hours listening to the service by loudspeaker.

Hundreds more were turned away as fire officials ordered auditorium doors locked.

Miss Kuhlman, a glamorous-looking woman in her fifties who combines the talents of a Billy Graham, an Oral Roberts

* *Minneapolis Star,* November 6, 1972

and an Aimée Semple McPherson, told the throng early she would not be responsible for "miracles" that would take place during the service.

"You do not need a Kathryn Kuhlman to touch you," she said. "It's the power and the presence of the Holy Spirit."

Throughout the service, while an organ played softly in the background, Miss Kuhlman reported "healings" she said were taking place in the auditorium.

"Someone behind me on the stage has a skin condition," she said. "He will find everything cleared up within three days."

"Dear Jesus," she said another time, "there is another cancer healing some place, and someone is getting an over-flow from it."

"Someone is being healed of a heart condition," she said later.

She invited those who had experienced the healings to come to the stage and "give praise to God."

She put her hands on the face of each person who came forward and invariably each collapsed "under the power of the Holy Spirit" into the arms of waiting aides. She appeared to give each a gentle nudge.

Scores of people claimed healings.

A woman in purple slacks from Austin, Minn., who said she had suffered for 15 years with two cracked discs swung her arms as hard as she could to demonstrate her recovery.

A 9-year-old boy from Hudson, Wis., who said he had a crippling ankle ailment, ran down an aisle.

A baker from Princeton, Minn., carried a brace he used to wear for cancer of the spine.

A woman who said she lived 60 miles from Chicago said she had four operations for a crippling disease but was able to leave the wheelchair and walk to the stage. When her wheelchair was lifted on to the stage, Miss Kuhlman instructed the woman to push her husband in it.

"He's been pushing you long enough," she said, observing: "You can't say it's psychomatic. It's the power of God."

A young woman from St. Paul who identified herself as "a Catholic Pentecostal" brought six Roman Catholic nuns to the stage with her.

One nun said she was healed of bursitis in a Kathryn Kuhlman service two years ago and was now "in perfect shape."

Miss Kuhlman, a Baptist who earlier had told about her recent visit to Pope Paul in the Vatican, reminded the audience, "We have the same Heavenly Father, the same High Priest."

Reflecting on the healings taking place in the auditorium, she said, "There's so much power in this place. So much glory."

She continued to identify the ills of people in the audience.

"There is somebody on the stage behind me with migraine headaches," she said. "Dear Jesus, I rebuke the migraines." Others, she said, had sinus, hearing and stomach problems, identifying the location in the auditorium of each.

Miss Kuhlman asked nearly every person who came to report healings what his church was.

After interviewing one excited person who said she was a Lutheran, Miss Kuhlman observed: "When a Lutheran shows this much emotion, you know it has to be of God . . . . This is going to happen in every Lutheran church in the country."

Miss Kuhlman introduced one man "with a brain tumor which impaired his vision and he's seeing perfectly now." . . .

"These healings have all been marvelous and glorious," said the evangelist, who frequently moved around the stage giving dramatic gestures. "They have been healed by the power of God.

"Some of you may not know it until you get home. Great has been the presence of the Holy Spirit. Great has been the glory of God in this place. Some may not know you have been healed until you've left this meeting.

"You've been thrilled as you watched these miracles. O beloved, there is a miracle far greater. You can well afford to live with a sick body, but you can't live a minute without your sins being forgiven. This is the most sacred part of the service."

Then she asked the persons who wanted to be "born again" to come to the front of the auditorium while she prayed for them.

Scores came and Miss Kuhlman led them in a prayer of confession while they stretched up their arms in "a token of surrender." Her soloist, Jimmy McDonald, sang "It's Well with My Soul," while the audience joined in.

"It would be a sacrilege to give a benediction at a service like this," Miss Kuhlman concluded. So she asked everyone to go out singing a revival hymn, "Hallelujah!"

"I pray that no one will leave this auditorium having seen Kathryn Kuhlman," she said.

After she dismissed the throng, many rushed forward to touch her.

Early in the service, Miss Kuhlman had pleaded with people: "Please do not touch me. You grieve me. I am the most ordinary person in the whole world. Reach up and touch Him," she said, referring to God.

"I do not lay hand upon people," she said. "I have no healing power in these hands."

Wearing a white sheath dress with billowy sleeves, she said she "never was God's first choice for a ministry like this. It's not a woman's work. It's a man's job I am doing."

In a choked voice, she recalled she was born in a town of 1,200 (Concordia, Mo.) and was "the most unlikely person in the whole world to be used of God."

One day, she said she had looked up and said, "Wonderful Jesus, I don't have a thing. If you can use this desolute life, use it and take it."

She said several times that she was frightened.

"I die a thousand deaths before I walk on this stage," she said. "You don't understand what it is like.

"You ask me why everyone is not healed. I don't know. If you think you have questions, I have more."

She said the basis of her ministry was the Word of God, lifting a Bible from the podium.

Miss Kuhlman's appearance here yesterday was sponsored by the charitable foundation that bears her name.

According to the *New York Times*, she takes a yearly salary of $25,000 plus travel expenses, turning over all other earnings to the foundation, which has built a hospital in Vietnam and distributed 1,200 wheelchairs to Vietnamese amputees. Her foundation has headquarters in Pittsburgh. Her programs are shown weekly on more than 60 television stations and broadcast on more than 50 radio stations.

Miss Kuhlman conducts weekly services in First Presbyterian Church, Pittsburgh, and makes monthly appearances at the Shrine Auditorium in Los Angeles.

Ushers and members of a massed choir for yesterday's service were recruited from local churches. They included singers from Soul's Harbor, who also sang separately. Several local clergymen sat on the stage with the choir.

In Miss Kuhlman's books, *I Believe in Miracles* and *God Can Do It Again*, doctors are quoted to substantiate various claims of dramatic healing.

At yesterday's service, she told members of the audience, "If you are a member of a medical association, feel free to examine any of these people being healed."

The following author is a widely published spokesman for the healing ministry in new Pentecostalism. He has a weekly column in the Pensacola (Florida) News Journal, *in which the question-answer format is used.*

Miracles and Healing*

I notice on your letterheads that you believe that bodily healing is in the atonement. Would you please explain this?

As Jesus bore our sins at Calvary, so He also bore our sicknesses on the cross. Matthew 8:16-17, "When the even was come, they brought unto Him (Jesus) many that were possessed with devils and He cast out the spirits with His Word and healed all that were sick: that it may be fulfilled which was spoken by Esaias the prophet saying, 'Himself took our infirmities and bare our sicknesses.'" This is a direct quote from Isaiah 53:5, which is a prophetic view of the sufferings of Christ. Jesus bore our sins (I Peter 2:24), and He bore our sicknesses (Matthew 8:16-17). The (full) gospel is that Jesus provides for the whole man through the benefits of the cross. The completion of this work in any part of man will not climax until the resurrection. However, we can appropriate the "earnest" of the redemption now by faith, i.e., forgiveness of sins and healing for our bodies (Mark 2).

Those who receive must believe for the benefits. As no sinner can be saved until he believes it is God's Will to save him and until he receives by faith, so no sick person can be healed until he believes it is God's Will to heal him and until he receives the benefits by faith. Scriptures that show how Jesus healed only those who believed for healing are: Matthew 8:8; 9:2; 9:27-30; 15:28; Mark 5:34; 10:52; Luke 17:19; John 4:47-53. The early church carried on this ministry of faith (John 14:12; Acts 14:8-10). Act now on what Jesus did for you and be healed.

---

* Ken Sumrall, *What's Your Question?* ($.95). Available from Whitaker Books, 504 Laurel Drive, Monroeville, Pa. 15146.

How do you answer those who say that the days of miracles are past?

These days of miracles are past for those who believe that they are. "According to your faith let it be unto you" (Matthew 9:29). "All things are possible to him that believeth" (Mark 9:23). "These signs shall follow them that believe . . ." (Mark 16:17).

"One article you wrote about three weeks ago about practicing religion instead of Bible Christianity was really appreciated. I know right here in Milton quite a few people, even in my own family, who are devout church goers on Sunday but leave their Christianity in the church the balance of the week. They are even taught by their ministers that other churches only practice doctrines—false, that is.

"Your article is the first I look for in Sunday papers. Our minister says there should be no antagonism between anyone's different religions and that is to me as it should be.

"So let's keep your picture with the articles in the paper."

Questions have come from many places concerning healing for our day. This week's answer is in the form of a testimony by our evangelist who is conducting revival services at Liberty Baptist Church—Brother T. W. McGraw.

I was a businessman in Biloxi, Mississippi, with over $100,000 business, owned an apartment house and had insurance to retire on when I reached sixty years of age. Then things began to happen.

My wife was given up as hopelessly incurable. My little girl was killed at a youth camp and my little boy got his neck broken. I suffered three nervous breakdowns, then took arthritis of the spine and cancer. I had to sleep in a chair for eight years, lived on dope for three and one-half years. The doctors said there was no medical cure for me. All they could do was give me shots to kill pain. Then I turned to God. He completely delivered me of every disease.

I lost all my business during the period of sickness. My

hospital bills were great. We lost our home and were given five days to move out. Those days were dark. I promised God to live for Him and serve Him. After weeks of fasting and prayer, God began to use me in the healing of the sick. Though I had never done any church work, calls began to come from churches for my services. Since 1963, I have seen many miracles and have led over 6,000 souls to Christ. I am not an ordained preacher. I just want to do my best for Jesus since He has done so much for me.

Do you believe it is God's Will to heal all the sick?

Since this subject causes contention among good people, I do not wish to add to the tension, which is a basic cause of sickness.

Therefore, I answer the question with "charity." We teach that Jesus bore our sins on the cross, and that He bore our sicknesses on the cross (I Peter 2:24; Matthew 8:17). The condition for receiving these benefits is faith (Ephesians 2:8; Matthew 9:29; Mark 11:22-24; 16:17; Acts 14:9 and James 5:15). On this basis, we pray for the sick in almost every service at Liberty Baptist Church. Not all are healed but many are, including those with heart disease, diabetes and cancer, I wish all were healed that we pray for. I am sure that more will be when we fully yield to the Holy Spirit to allow God's Love to flow more freely among us. As long as many are being healed and God's Word seems to endorse praying for the sick, we shall continue by God's help to minister to the needs of those who come.

If you can heal the sick, why don't you empty out the hospitals? This would certainly prove that your healing ministry is genuine.

In the first place, I don't claim to heal the sick. I simply obey the Lord and pray for them if they desire prayer and believe that Jesus heals the body in this day. Even Jesus said, "According to your faith, let it be unto you" (Matthew 9:29).

I wish I knew more about healing the sick, but as long as some are being healed through the laying on of hands and prayer of faith, I believe it is worthwhile to continue the healing ministry. Many testimonies are available from those who have been healed at Liberty Baptist Church of deafness, heart disease, cancer, and many other diseases.

This is an excellent summary by Sumrall of the New Pentecostal understanding of demonology.

Demons*

Do you believe in the existence of demons?

The word "demon" is not found in the King James Version of the Bible, but wherever the word "devils" is found it should be translated "demons." There is one "devil" but many "demons." An example in Matthew 8:16: ". . . they brought unto him (Jesus) many that were possessed with devils (demons) and he cast out the spirits with His Word, and healed all that were sick."

Many have denied the existence of demons or evil spirits, but to do so is to deny the Scriptures. Jesus cast over 2,000 demons out of one man (Mark 5:1-15). Mary Magdalene was delivered of seven devils (Luke 8:2).

The early church also cast out devils according to the word of Jesus (Mark 16:17-18). Philip cast out devils and they came out crying with loud voices (Acts 8). Paul cast devils out of a woman in Philippi (Acts 16).

I do not believe that we are to go on a demon search, or to become "demon-conscious." Demons will manifest themselves in the presence of the Holy Spirit (Mark 1:23-26). We are to be aware that demons exist and learn how to combat them (Ephesians 6:10-18).

* Ken Sumrall, *What's Your Question?* ($.95). Available from Whitaker Books, 504 Laurel Drive, Monroeville, Pa. 15146.

As in Bible days, many today are possessed with unclean spirits, infirm spirits, and countless others. These tormenting spirits are causing mental and physical sickness. The Holy Spirit has been given to the Church to bring deliverance to these oppressed people (Mark 16:17-18; Acts 10:38).

I have many questions in my mind concerning demons. Can a Christian be possessed or deceived by demons? How can you tell if a person has demons? If he has them, how do you deal with them?

Since most Christians are fearful of "ghosts" which cannot be seen, they have chosen to ignore the Scriptures which speak of evil spirits or they simply attribute the Scriptural statements about demons to the superstitions of ignorant people. There are others who attribute every personal problem to evil spirits. Some of these people become demon-conscious and are quick to label people as "demon-possessed."

I feel that both of these positions are harmful to the cause of Christ.

The Scripture declares that we are not to be ignorant of Satan's devices (II Corinthians 2:11). We are to be on guard against evil spirits and be alert to their deceiving methods (Ephesians 6:10-12; I Peter 5:8-9). However, we must be aware that some problems of the inner man are caused by what the Scripture calls "flesh" or "old man" (Galatians 5:17-21). Before we begin discerning evil spirits in others, we must be willing to allow others to apply the same set of standards on us that we use on them. If you are not willing for others to diagnose all of your ugly dispositions as evil spirits, then be very sure you treat others as you would want to be treated. Jesus did not commission us to go "witch hunting." He did give us power to cast out devils when we discern them (Mark 16:17).

To answer your question about demons possessing or deceiving Christians, I shall distinguish between "possessing" and "deceiving." If the definition of possession is "to be controlled by" then I would say that no Christian can be completely controlled by evil spirits. However, certain areas of a Christian's life may be strongly influenced and controlled by demon forces. Just because a person is indwelt by the Holy Spirit does not mean the Spirit completely controls him. There would be no need for the strong admonitions of the New Testament to be on the alert if it is not possible for evil spirits to invade the life of a believer. When Dr. V. Raymond Edmor of Wheaton College was asked the question you asked, he answered, "Theory says no, but the facts say yes. It is theoretical that a demon cannot possess a body in which the Holy Spirit dwells. However, I know true Christians who were delivered from demons in answer to prayer given in the Name of the Lord Jesus."

It is explicitly stated in the Scriptures that all people are deceived by the Devil until they are born again (Ephesians 2:1-3; Titus 3:5; II Corinthians 4:4). When the person rejects Satan's ways and claims Jesus Christ as his Lord, the glorious light of the gospel shines into his heart and he becomes a child of God. God's Nature is planted in his spirit. He begins a new life (II Peter 1:3; II Corinthians 5:17). What causes much confusion in believers is the fact that his mind and body are not instantly redeemed. There must be a constant renewal of the mind (Ephesians 4:23; Romans 12:1-3). A believer also needs to be filled with the Holy Spirit so that he can be led into ALL truth and equipped with power to overcome the wicked spirits.

The answer to the question about Christians being deceived is—yes, they can and often are. Those who do not judge their own thoughts by the Word of God are subject to be deceived. Our minds are like large living rooms into which evil spirits come without invitation. All truth, learned or revealed, comes from God. Every lie, learned or revealed, comes from Satan. Jesus said, "Ye shall know the truth and the truth shall set you free" (John 8:32). On the other hand if what you know is a lie, then to that degree you are not free. You can see the importance of knowing God's Word. The first piece of armour mentioned in fighting evil spirits is "truth" (Ephesians 6:14). If our hearts are full of God's Word (Truth) then we can readily discern thoughts given by evil spirits. These thoughts which enslave, defile, and torment are from demons. If they invade the living room of your mind, cast them out by rebuking them in Jesus' Name and by pleading the Blood of Jesus. In order to stay free, renounce all evil and make a total commitment of your body, soul, and spirit unto the Lord Jesus Christ (I Corinthians 12:10).

Do you believe demons exercise greater activity in some areas more than in other areas?

Definitely, yes. In pagan countries where few know the Lord Jesus Christ, there is very little opposition to demon powers. Missionaries who have ministered in pagan countries can vouch for strange manifestations of demon powers and the terrible oppressive spirit of some areas. Many people in the world ignorantly worship Satan and his demon forces (I Corinthians 10:20-21). For example, in oriental countries some people think they are worshipping spirits of their ancestors, when actually they are worshipping evil spirits.

For many years there was little demon activity in this nation as compared with heathen nations. The Bible was read in almost every classroom. This nation, though never entirely Christian, had a respect for God, the Bible, and morality. However, with the removal of the Bible and prayer from our schools and homes, the Devil has gained much strength in our land. Many people are being oppressed and possessed by demon forces all over the USA. I believe there is a definite connection between demons and the spreading of such drugs as LSD, speed, amphetamines, etc. There is also a connection in the crime wave, violence, homosexuality, long hair on males and demon activity. Since we have always associated demon activity with paganism, we must define paganism. The best way I know to define it is by its fruits, which are: lawlessness, nudity, rock and roll music in a minor key, sexual perversion, and ignorance of the Bible. These things are prevalent in all barbarian lands. America is fast becoming pagan and is in need of deliverance. It is the responsibility of God's people to rise up and declare the power of Jesus' Name and His Blood to set men free from these demonic forces (Revelation 12:11). The main reason for the present-day move of the Holy Spirit is to restore the body of Christ to the supernatural power of its early days so as to raise up a standard against the flood of the enemy (Isaiah 59:19). The answer is not Washington marches; nor is it psychiatry, education, or just the letter of God's Word. The answer is the full gospel delivered under the anointing of the Holy Spirit. Amen and amen!

How does a person cast out demons that are in another person?

1. Do not attempt to enter this ministry without training in the wiles of the Devil and unless you can discern evil spirits. All believers have authority over demons, but all do not have discernment nor are they spiritually ready for this ministry (Matthew 17:20-21). 2. Be sure that the person desires deliverance. If he doesn't, then pray for a change of his mind. 3. Make the person who desires deliverance understand Satan's defeat at Calvary and convince him of the Victory that is in Jesus Christ. (I have noticed that some keep reminding Satan of his defeat. That is unnecessary since he already knows and trembles when others realize it [James 2:19]. Satan knows when you are convinced, and also when you are bluffing.) There is no magic formula for casting out evil spirits. The sons of Sceva tried this method and miserably failed (Acts 19). Your faith in what Jesus has done brings victory when you speak the word of faith.

4. Be filled with the Holy Spirit. Jesus cast out demons by the Spirit of God (Matthew 12:28). 5. Boldly quote the Words of God against Satan as Jesus did (Matthew 4). Remember, however, that the Word of God is the sword of the Spirit and not our own sword. The anointing breaks the yoke (Isaiah 10:27; Luke 4:18). 6. Say: "In the Name of Jesus Christ, I command you evil spirits to depart." Stand your ground without wavering. Evil spirits know that they must submit to a Spirit-filled person who knows he has authority in the Name of Jesus (Mark 6:7). Expect them to leave. THEY WILL! Victory is certain through our resurrected Lord.

The new Pentecostal teachings and practices about demons and healings have been widely criticized or even riduculed because, as Morton T. Kelsey shows in his new book, Healing and Christianity, *these run directly contrary to the attitudes of most Americans and western Europeans about medicine. The task of the latter is simply to heal the body, which is a physical mechanism which responds to treatment. Every patient is a combination of organs and physical processes who can be treated by a wide variety of medical procedures such as diets, drugs, surgery. Only a handful of physicians, clergymen, and laity believe that the mind and emotions of the patient can be effectively ministered to by those trained in this field. Hence, most Christians think of Pentecostal teachings about demons, exorcism, and healing as being far removed from sound, scientific thinking.*

In its thoughtful study in 1970 of the entire new Pentecostal movement, the appointed study commission of the United Presbyterian Church in the United States of America faced these questions and reached the conclusions stated in the following selection.

Healing and Exorcism of Demons*

Another dimension in the discussion of the work of the Holy Spirit in the Church today is found in the phenomenon

* Report of the Special Committee on the Work of the Holy Spirit, United Presbyterian Church in the United States of America.

known as exorcism, that ancient rite by which satanic forces called demons, including Satan himself on occasion, are called forth from their possessive clutch upon an individual life.

There are three accounts of special significance in the life of Jesus when he encounters this demonic force. The accounts are particularly memorable because the Gospels record them in some detail.

One is that dreadful experience of testing which Jesus underwent in the Judean wilderness. He must have told the experience to his followers in vivid terms because they remembered it so well. They had no other way in which they could have learned of it because he was alone. There was no one else present to witness the occasion. Jesus clearly thought of it as a crucial turning point in his time of trials, for the nature of his testing reflects a basic questioning of his destiny, his vocation, and his identity.

The other two occasions which are especially noteworthy are the times when Jesus meets an epileptic boy brought to him by the father of the child, and the unforgettably vivid encounter between Jesus and the madman from the tombs of the Gadarene country.

The Gospels tell us about "unclean spirits," the disciples are sent forth to "cast out demons," among other commissions given to them. John's Gospel tells us that the devil is "the Father of Lies," and that he entered into Judas.

How are we to interpret these evidences in the life of Jesus of his recognition of demonic spirits? Shall we dismiss the problem by saying it is only a question of terminology? Or, shall we allegorize the occasions of demonic possession? Or, shall we conclude that the accounts represent a cultural limitation, reflecting the limited knowledge of the period? Or, shall we say flatly that what the New Testament calls demon possession we would probably call neuroses or psychotic states of being? And in the wilderness, shall we say that the adversary whom Jesus met in the story is a personification of evil?

Each of these conclusions is possible, and each represents a facet of the many-sided problem of demon possession; but what no amount of demythologizing can do is to discount the possibility that Jesus saw a dark reality which we often miss in our devotion to rationality, important as reason clearly is for any mature understanding of the Christian faith.

Is it not conceivable that beyond the testing of his nature and the uses of his powers, Jesus saw something more? Can we not assume that beneath the outward appearance of illness and psychoses, Jesus sometimes perceived a malignant force at work whose purpose was ever to bring sickness where there was health, division where there was wholeness, and death where there was life? Does it not seem likely that the one in whom truth and life were united in an unprecedented singleness of will should be extraordinarily perceptive about that which is the enemy of truth and life? Might it not be true that Jesus saw illness as clearly and accurately as we see it, both emotional and physical, but that he saw something else in some instances, a shadow behind the divisiveness, an adversary, an anti-Christ?

If the implication of these questions be true, it is of great importance that we observe the calm, unquestioned authority with which Jesus meets that malignant presence. There is never any sign of struggle in which there is a doubt about who the victor will be. With assurance, Jesus commands, "Get thee behind me, Satan," and with utter simplicity, he restores the Gadarene man to his rightful mind, and heals the demonic boy. It is never a question of dualistic division between the forces of darkness and the legions of light. Jesus is the Lord and wherever he meets that which is contrary to his love and Truth, he quietly overcomes it, as do his disciples. "Lord," they said on their return, "even the demons were subject to us." And since that time, there have been others among us who, by the power of the Holy Spirit, have also claimed to have the power of the Holy Spirit to cast out demons.

However, there are grave dangers in such practices. The history of the church is filled with those who have used Satan as a convenient escape from responsibility. To attribute angry and hostile feelings to the devil is to be freed from having to face the truth within oneself about where those feelings come from and what one must do to overcome them. To blame the adversary for the blight and burden of poverty, militarism, and racism is to cut the nerve of reformation and progress.

Moreover, to be looking for the devil in every situation of life is to commit oneself to an unhealthy quagmire of blame and judgment in personal relationships which presently alienates one from the human family, with the result that the devil has only served the devil, "and the last state is worse than the first."

These dangers are so real and prevalent that there appears to be little usefulness served in encouraging any practice which would excuse human faults by blaming a personal devil. The belief, though representative of a reality in the experience of contemporary man, · as well as the men of the New Testament, is so subject to distortion and misuse that wisdom would seem to encourage the most careful approach. There is ample explanation in the complexities and conflicts in all of us for the evil we do. Yet no man who has looked long and hard at the intractable, abysmal depth of human iniquity can deny that there is at least a shadow of an evil reality beyond human life.

Perhaps the only practical criterion we can follow is that of hard and constant day-labor against evil in all its multiplicity, personal and social, leaving the matter of its origin and nature to the mind of God.

This selection outlines the important teachings by a careful Catholic Pentecostal scholar about Satan and demons.

Warring Against the Evil One*

It is characteristic of the Pentecostal movement that, along with renewed faith in the Holy Spirit, there comes a greater awareness of the evil spirit. Perhaps this is because a keener spiritual sensitivity makes a person more perceptive of evil influences as well as good ones. Perhaps it is because, when the Holy Spirit begins to act in a more manifest way, Satan retaliates by doing likewise. (May it not be that the widespread modern disbelief in the reality of the devil is simply a counterpart of the modern neglect of the Holy Spirit?)

In any case, experience has taught people in the Pentecostal movement to take very seriously that aspect of the Christian life that has to do with warring against the evil one. One very intellectual leader of the Pittsburgh community, of decidedly liberal tendencies, used to maintain that Satan was only a mythical expression for the dark forces latent in human nature. Not long after the events of February and March, 1967, someone asked him whether he believed in Satan now. "You better believe I do," he replied—laughing, but dead serious. The Epistle to the Ephesians is not pursuing a myth, but is giving solid, practical counsel when it warns us:

We are not contending against flesh and blood, but against the principalities, against the powers, against the world rulers of this present darkness, against the spiritual hosts of wickedness in the heavenly places (Eph. 6:12; cf. I Pet. 5:8).

Many of the prayer communities, including those in Pittsburgh, South Bend, Lansing and Ann Arbor, have had some

---

* Edward D. O'Connor, *The Pentecostal Movement in the Catholic Church* (Notre Dame: Ave Maria Press, 1971), pp. 79-80.

frightening encounters with the work of Satan. The stories will not be told here, for it seems unhealthy to dwell on such incidents. There is already a tendency in some places to pay too much attention to the diabolic. It is not unhealthy, however, to bear in mind the true nature of the enemy with whom we are contending.

Since the earliest days in Pittsburgh, it has been a common practice within the movement to exorcise Satan any time there seems to be reason to fear his influence. In many places this is done quite regularly before a person is prayed over for the baptism in the Spirit. Ordinarily no set formula is used. The one leading the prayer simply invokes the power of Christ in whatever terms he sees fit, and in his name commands Satan to depart and give place to the Holy Spirit.

Study Guide Questions for Chapter 8

1. As modern medicine continues to make such rapid progress, why do so many persons continue to accept the faith-healing ministry?

2. Despite the fact that trained observers believe new Pentecostalists to be as mentally healthy as nonparticipants, do you think those who speak in tongues, practice faith healing, and exorcise demons are out of step with man's ability to understand his problems through reason, intelligence, and common sense?

3. In what manner might a belief in the power of Satan to create evil in this world be an impediment to social progress? Do you believe the new Pentecostalist belief in demons to be such an impediment?

9. The Further Gifts of the Spirit

While tongues, healing, and exorcism of demons are the most controversial gifts of the Baptism in the Holy Spirit, they constitute only some of the gifts promised in I Corinthians 12. This chapter presents a brief description of the further gifts, none of which are as spectacular as those already discussed, but all being considered by new Pentecostalists to be of equal weight for use in the charismatic community. Note especially the discussion by Donald L. Gelpi, S.J., below, that the gifts must not be limited only to the nine in I Corinthians, but include all "true acts of piety." This is, indeed, a marked theological departure from the teachings of the older Pentecostalism.

This is a brief recapitulation and explanation of the gifts with special attention to those not already discussed in this handbook.

A Summary of the Nine Gifts*

1. *The Word of Wisdom.* In a difficult or dangerous situation, a Christian will be given a word of wisdom which solves the problem, or silences an opponent. This is not the same as the wisdom which an individual has acquired through experience. It is, rather, a "word" of wisdom, which will be given to various members of the congregation according to need.

2. *The Word of Knowledge.* This gift reveals facts from the natural or supernatural world, which a Christian would not be able to know by normal means.

3. *Faith.* This is not the "faith unto salvation" which every Christian has, nor the "fruit of the Spirit" (Gal. 5:22),

* Reprinted by permission from *Speaking in Tongues,* by Larry Christenson, published and copyright 1968, Bethany Fellowship, Inc., Minneapolis, Minnesota 55438.

which every Christian should bring forth, but this is "mountain-moving faith" (Matt. 17:20; I Cor. 13:2), which individual Christians may manifest as a gift of the Spirit.

4. *Healing.* The main thrust of this gift is toward the healing of the body from physical infirmity. Beyond that, however, it would apply to the healing of "the whole man" —body, soul and spirit.

5. *Miracles.* This gift goes beyond the miraculous healing of the body to include miracles of every sort. The object of the miracle is determined by the situation and need of the moment.

6. *Prophecy.* The primary emphasis in this gift is not upon prediction of future events, but upon an appropriate and needed word in the present situation—a word of up-building, encouragement, consolation (I Cor. 14:3). This word, of course, may well include a glance either into the past or into the future.

7. *Discernment of Spirits.* This gift enables the Church of Christ and her members to distinguish between divine, human, and demonic powers—to discern the source of a particular utterance or action.

8. *Speaking in Tongues.* Through this gift, the exalted Lord gives the members of His Church the power to "express the inexpressible," and praise God in new speech.

9. *Interpretation.* This is a "sister gift" which makes it possible and useful for the gift of tongues to be used in a group meeting. Interpretation is not an exact "translation" of the utterance in tongues, nor a commentary upon it, but is a rendering in the vernacular of the content or "gist" of the utterance in tongues. The one who speaks in tongues speaks to God; the one who interprets receives the interpretation from God.

Consider with what absolute legitimacy one might earnestly desire and seek any one of these gifts, motivated by love. If there is someone in the congregation who is confused and uncertain about the truth of the Gospel, or who has a personal problem, what more loving thing could you do than deliver to such a one the Spirit's word of wisdom for that particular need? If the congregation is in a state of spiritual lethargy or disillusionment, what more loving thing could you do than deliver to them a prophetic word—an exhortation from the Spirit? If a member is sick, what more loving thing could you do than deliver to him the healing power of Christ? If the congregation is under pointed attack by the principalities and powers, the spiritual hosts of wickedness, what more loving thing could you do than to discern their presence, and with the authority of the Name of Jesus stand against them? Yes, even the gift of tongues: If you are called to edify the congregation, what more loving thing could you do than first go into your private prayer closet and let the Lord edify you—speak ten thousand words in a tongue, if need be—so that when you come to church you will be so edified that five words with the mind will be spiritual dynamite. This is the logical way to interpret St. Paul's words in I Corinthians 14:18-19: "I thank God that I speak in tongues more than you all; nevertheless, in church I would rather speak five words with my mind, in order to instruct others, than ten thousand in a tongue."

Because he loved, St. Paul spoke in tongues more than them all. He knew that in this gift God had given him a supernatural tool for edification. Faithfully used, it would enable him better to guide and edify those under his charge. But because it was love which motivated him—and not the desire to show off spiritually—this gift was one which he used primarily, perhaps exclusively, in his private worship. Whatever the Lord wrought in private would inevitably bless the churches as Paul continued to move among them in his appointed calling.

It is not too much to say that there is a direct ratio between love and desire: The greater place which the love of Christ has in our hearts, the greater will be our desire for the gifts of the Spirit, through which we may effectively express that love.

Manifestation

When the Body of Christ is functioning in a normal way —normal by New Testament standards—the gifts of the Spirit which Paul lists in I Corinthians 12 will come into manifestation . . . as they are needed. Our key to understanding and visualizing the way in which this works is in verse 7: "To each is given the manifestation of the Spirit for the common good." The picture given us is this: The Holy Spirit has a supply of gifts. He gives these to various members of the congregation. But the gift is not for the private benefit of the one who receives it: The member is a "manifester" of the gift. He holds it in trust, and at the proper time administers it, for the benefit of the Body. He receives it in order to manifest it—deliver it—to the one for whom it is ultimately intended. Only when it comes to that person does it become, in the true sense, a "gift."

Consider, for example, a person who is sick. The Spirit gives, or has given, "gifts of healing" to a member of the congregation. This person goes to the sick member and manifests the gift which the Spirit has entrusted to him— and the sick person receives healing.

The word of wisdom and the word of knowledge operate in a similar way. The gift, as we have seen, is not designated "wisdom" or "knowledge" per se, but a word (or "utterance") of wisdom or knowledge. The person who manifests one of these gifts has received a word or an utterance. By the Spirit, he has been granted momentary access to a tiny segment of God's infinite wisdom or knowledge. To the one who manifests it, it may seem a rather ordinary "word" —a thought, idea, or illustration which is impressed upon his mind. But for the one who receives it—the one for whom it is intended—it is truly a word of wisdom or a word of knowledge.

The Holy Spirit broods over the flock of God with watchful eye, determining with absolute wisdom the need of each member, as well as the needs of the group, and then gives gifts to meet those needs—to the extent that He finds members yielded to His moving, ready to manifest the gifts which He apportions as He wills.

This is an excellent, concise summary of the further gifts, noteworthy for its restraint as contrasted to the more boastful interpretations of these gifts exhibited by the old Pentecostalists.

The Gifts of Wisdom, Knowledge, Faith, Prophecy, and Discernment*

The Word of Wisdom

Foremost among the gifts which the Spirit bestows is wisdom. There is an attitude of childlike simplicity which opens us to these gifts. In entering into our new life, we often experience these realities like small children. Groping, searching, still in awe at the wonder of it all—it is no accident that the gift of tongues, that childlike babble, is therefore the first gift usually experienced. The other gifts of the Spirit, especially such an exalted one as wisdom, being less spectacular, we discover as we begin to toddle around. In fact very often we find we've been "playing with" it for some time but did not know its name. This is our experience with the word of wisdom. In the first few weeks and months of this pentecostal "outburst," one ability, one power seemed to be very evident in a few individuals. We came to call this (for want of a better name) the "gift of inspired preaching." That's what it was. But it was also the word of wisdom

---

* Kevin and Dorothy Ranaghan, *Catholic Pentecostals* (Paramus, N.J.: Paulist Newman Press, 1969), pp. 162-76.

unrecognized as such. When one of these individuals stood before a group to proclaim the Good News of Christ, there was a piercing, penetrating quality to his words which struck the root, the core of every listener. We had heard the same words before; we had in many cases heard the same speaker before; but now into his proclamation came a new dynamism, a new conviction, a new penetration, which hushed and stirred us all.

Wisdom is not particularly exotic, alluring or exciting. As a spoken word it carries the peace, the will, and the authority of the Lord. It may be missed. In our stumbling way as we began to walk in the way of the Spirit, using these gifts, we began to refer to every gift of utterance as prophecy—which, of course, it was, using "prophecy" in the broadest sense of the term. For example we knew that when a problem arose in the community and an important decision had to be made, if we would gather to pray the Lord would speak through us to give light and direction. At one point amid the confusion and ramblings someone would speak forth, and immediately from that point onward there would be no need to seek further. We knew that without it being infallible the "supremely right thing" had just been said, and the task now became clear. All actions should carry out the plan that had been spoken. We have come to expect that gift to be operative when we meet for such important decisions. We got in the habit of praying during such meetings for a "prophecy" from the Lord for direction. When it came, we knew it. But what we now begin to see, is that when it came it was the "word of wisdom."

In Acts 6, 1-5, the apostles had a similar meeting for a problem which had arisen in the community, and we have an example of the word of wisdom operating. "Now in those days as the number of disciples was increasing, there arose a murmuring among the Hellenists against the Hebrews that their widows were being neglected in the daily ministration. So the Twelve called together the multitude of the disciples and said, 'It is not right that we should give up preaching the word of God and serve tables. Therefore, brethren, pick out from among you seven men of good repute, full of the Spirit and of wisdom, whom we may appoint to this duty. But we will devote ourselves to prayer and to the ministry of the word.' And what they said pleased the whole multitude . . ." That plan which meets the approval of the "whole multitude," that penetrating word which shows clearly what the Lord would have us do, that word which cuts us to the heart with its truth and might—that is the word of wisdom.

It is one gift which is obviously very closely related to gifts of preaching, leadership and counsel in the community. This wisdom we speak of is not an abiding personal characteristic (the "naturally" sagacious man). It is more than a permanent human talent, yet it certainly is grounded in and thrives upon a strong foundation of knowledge, prudence and familiarity with the word of God. And it remains a gift of utterance. It speaks a word to one moment and to no other. When it is heard, "something happens." To all who have ears, "let them hear."

The Word of Knowledge

Interpreters vary in their attempts to determine exactly what Saint Paul means by the various gifts of the Spirit. This is especially true of "the word of knowledge." Our "probable" opinion comes from experience—where it seems to have both an individual and communal level of operation. In the former case it closely resembles the gift of discernment at first glance, but it is different in operation. Many times, for example, we would find ourselves with a stranger and after only minutes the knowledge of what they needed to hear would be on our lips. Suddenly, inexorably, we would see to the root of the need or the problem of a person. When spoken, this is indeed a word of knowledge, but since the gifts are given not only to individuals but to the Church, for the Church, it becomes obvious that the more frequent exercise of this gift will be ecclesial in nature. Its function is to speak the word of knowledge to all in the community here and now. It is no wonder then that we see a close connection between this gift and the gift of teaching. This is not to say that all teaching in the Church involves this gift. (Would that it did!) But once again this gift, when present, is known. It is recognized. We will recognize it as long as we are not looking for thunder and lightning. A gentle rain can water the parched earth as well as a cloudburst. If we are unable to see the manifestations of the Spirit unless they are spectacular, we may miss them altogether. Over and over again we have found in our gatherings that, as with the word of wisdom when the word of knowledge is spoken, the truths may be old, the speaker the same, and yet at that moment the lesson sinks in, penetrates, confounds and refreshes as never before. At that moment the quality, tone, presentation, and content is such that we can only describe it in the terminology of our evangelical brothers. It is "anointed." "When the Spirit of truth comes, he will guide you into all the truth" (Jn. 16, 13).

Faith

To respond, to listen, to accept the word of God initially is in itself a gift of God. The faith, the choice, the radical commitment of ourselves to Jesus is a leap of love. Why then is faith listed as a consequence of our response and acceptance? Faith that says "yes" to Jesus initially need be only a quiet "amen" to the call of God. With that the Lord can work. But the faith that serves a charismatic function is quite different. It is the faith of Job, unshakable in the midst of adversity, of Abraham in the face of absurdity, of Peter setting his foot on the water. It is faith that dares to believe that God will be true to his Word no matter how impossible the situation.

Consider this example from Acts: "Now Peter and John were going up to the temple at the hour of prayer, the ninth hour. And a man lame from birth was being carried, whom they laid daily at the gate of the temple which is called Beautiful to ask alms of those who entered the temple. Seeing Peter and John about to go into the temple, he asked for alms. And Peter directed his gaze at him, with John, and said, 'Look at us.' And he fixed his attention upon them, expecting to receive something from them. But Peter said, 'I have no silver and gold, but I give you what I have; in the name of Jesus Christ of Nazareth, walk'" (Acts 3, 1-6).

What is important here is not the miracle, not the healing (for the beggar did arise and walk). What we should see here is the gift of faith that Peter had to have to be able to believe that God would heal this man. It is easy to say "I believe God can heal." It is quite another thing to say faith which dares to believe the ultimate and to claim it is a gift of the Spirit. Such faith on the part of even one person in a community can uplift, can edify, can strengthen and sustain the rest. It is a gift of great power.

Prophecy

Unique and yet united to all the gifts of utterance is prophecy. The everyday understanding of what it means to be a prophet is a sorry mixture of fortune telling and extra-sensory perception. Yet the notion of a prophet being one who predicts the future is far from biblical. The word "prophet" comes from the Hebrew *nabi* or the Greek *prophetes* which means "he who speaks for, or on behalf of." In this we see that a prophet reveals the future only insofar as he is like a weatherman. The weatherman looks at the present, deeply, knowingly, draws from past experience and can "see" that snow will fall tomorrow. In the gift of prophecy, an estimation of our religious situation necessarily involves an ability to know and to interpret the present deeply and to see in it the dynamism and the movement of the future. In the divine sphere this makes Jesus the prophet par excellence, for he is the supreme utterance, the perfect Word who speaks for the Godhead to us. He is the divine communication as human person. In him is all past, present and future; as Karl Rahner says:

"Though in him divine revelation has come to a close, prophets still have their para-institutional place in the Church, because ever and ever again there are people in the Church divinely sent to it to bear a personal testimony to the reality of God and Christ in the might of his Spirit."

This testimony is at times the embodied witness of a lifetime. These are the real prophets. Yet in this instance we are referring to prophetic utterance, to a word-gift given for a moment to an individual. The individual is not necessarily a prophet therefore, but he sometimes exercises a decided gift for prophecy, a gift for speaking out in the Lord's name as he is prompted. The word of prophecy is the word of the Lord to a particular situation, perhaps to edify, encourage, console, or to teach, but always to ignite, enflame and enkindle. Prophetic utterance is meant to give a balance to the other Word-gifts. To the light of wisdom and knowledge, prophecy adds fire.

Since Jesus is *the* revelation of God to man, all prophecy, all teaching and all knowledge of him have their root and source of origin in the word of God. Scripture molds the content of any truly inspired utterance no matter what form it takes in being spoken. This is no doubt why the sound of "prophesying" from the mouth of an Evangelical Christian sounds strange to us. The message is the Lord's, but the medium is the King James Version of the bible. Therefore each sentence begins with "Yea I say unto thee" and usually ends with "Thus saith the Lord." In yielding to the prompting to speak forth a "prophetic" message, a Catholic in the same situation is more likely to use the language of contemporary texts. "Don't you know . . ." "The Lord would say," etc.

Forms through which the Lord would speak to us may be unfamiliar, but the authentic message from God will always ring true. How will we know? Are we sure it is the Lord? How can we test a genuine prophecy? Doesn't the weatherman make a mistake sometimes? In the spiritual realm, rain, when all signs point to sunshine, is most undesirable. The test of the prophetic utterance is found in its accord with the word of God.

"Beloved, do not believe every spirit, but test the spirits to see whether they are of God; for many false prophets have gone out into the world. By this you know the Spirit of God: every spirit which confesses that Jesus Christ has come in the flesh is of God, and every spirit which does not confess Jesus is not of God" (I Jn. 4, 1-3). "Therefore I want you to understand that no one speaking by the Spirit of God ever says 'Jesus be cursed!' and no one can say 'Jesus is Lord' except by the Holy Spirit" (I Cor. 12, 3). " 'Beware of false prophets, who come to you in sheep's clothing but inwardly are ravenous wolves. You will know them by their fruits' " (Mt. 7, 15-16).

Discernment of Spirits

The interrelationships among the gifts again become obvious when we talk of "testing the spirits" of the prophets. Again it becomes clear that the Lord never gives a burdensome gift. Should the exercise of one gift raise problems, another gift is given to help.

The gift of "discernment" is not a propensity on the part

of one person to tell everyone else just what is wrong with them. We have seen some harm done in the name of "discernment" over what was in actuality a "difference." We, for example, do not like the more emotional manifestations which occasionally accompany the working of the Lord in an individual. Laughing, crying, trembling—how immediately, how easily we want to say that it is not "of God." Perhaps it is not, but our judgment must come from the Lord and not be grounded merely on our tastes or likes.

Contradiction in the life of the Spirit is impossible. We have already been warned by the Lord not to judge lest we ourselves be judged. True discernment is not merely a keen insight into the workings of our all too frail human nature. . . . Discernment as a gift from God is the ability to distinguish at one moment in time whether the spirit behind a particular person, place, event, action, or situation is "of God" or not. It is obvious that if the work of God is to proceed, such a gift, acting as an agent of correction or counsel, is invaluable. We have seen that prudence and a great deal of care must be exercised by the individual who initially finds himself "aware" of these realities by the power of this gift. Holiness is no prerequisite to the reception of the gifts, nor is maturity. Yet where either is sorely lacking, the gifts can quickly become misused. In a community of love, this gift comes to take its place and perspective in the life in the Spirit.

The following is an extremely important expression of the teaching that the Baptism in the Holy Spirit bestows charisms or gifts far more extensive than the original nine.

The Doctrine of the Gifts*

4.2 The charismatic experience finds expression in a variety of spiritual gifts which are granted by the Holy Spirit

* Donald L. Gelpi, *Pentecostalism: A Theological Viewpoint* (Paramus, N.J.: Paulist Newman Press, 1971).

for the benefit of the entire community. The Corinthians seem to have manifested an excessive preoccupation with certain charismatic gifts, like speaking in tongues. Paul attempts to counteract this morbid concern with a more balanced attitude. Several points in his handling of the problem are of interest.

4.22 Every true act of piety, however seemingly insignificant, is a gift proceeding from the Spirit of Christ. Paul warns the community that the simplest profession of faith that "Jesus is Lord" is impossible unless one possesses the Spirit of Christ (1 Cor. 12:1-3). One cannot, therefore, regard praying in tongues alone, prophecy, or miracles as the only gifts granted by the Spirit. In his own catalogue of gifts Paul also includes "helpers," "leaders" and "teachers." The essential thing is, therefore, to see the life of the community as possessing an organic unity guided by the Spirit.

4.21 The same Spirit is the source of every gift, great or small. No single individual possesses all the gifts of the Spirit. The fact that different individuals possess different gifts is a sign that a particular individual is granted a charism in order to use it for the benefit of those who do not possess the same gift. The variety of gifts has as its purpose, therefore, to foster mutual service and love in the Spirit (1 Cor. 12:4-30).

7.221 There is no complete catalogue of the gifts of the Spirit; instead the Spirit apportions his gifts according to each individual's needs and the needs of the community. The catalogue of charisms in 1 Corinthians corresponds only roughly to the catalogues which appear in other letters of Paul (1 Cor 12:8 ff, 28 ff; Rom 12:6 ff; Eph 4:11; cf. 1 Pet 4:11). Of those listed, certain charisms pertain specifically to community leaders: apostles, leaders, evangelists, teachers, doctors, etc. It seems not unlikely, then, that Paul's carelessness in his enumeration of the gifts of the Spirit results at least in part from his awareness that the Spirit is capable of bestowing an endless variety of gifts. Those which he enumerates, therefore, give a good indication of the services and the expression of piety practiced in the apostolic community.

Most exegetes agree that the so-called "hymn" to love in the thirteenth chapter of 1 Corinthians is a later insert into the original text, possibly from another letter of Paul. Its doctrinal content is, however, certainly Pauline. The passage re-inforces the reflections which open chapter fourteen.

Paul faults the members of the Corinthian community for having failed to use their charisms as an expression of love. At the same time he does not demand that they choose between love and the other gifts of the Spirit, but only that they value love more than any single gift and that they use whatever gifts they have as an expression of love.

It is in this context that Paul's regulations for praying in tongues at community gatherings should be interpreted. The regulations concern a specific community which manifested disturbing tendencies. As a result the community was experiencing serious difficulty in discerning the "spirits" which moved its members. It should also be noted that before setting down specific rules regulating the exercise of specific charisms at meetings, Paul, with typical modesty, admits to having "a greater gift of tongues than all of you." Nevertheless he expresses his personal preference for modes of expression at community gatherings which will be a benefit to the entire community and which will serve to edify even the unbaptized who attend community meetings out of curiosity and interest. He attempts to check the community's morbid fascination with tongue-speaking by restricting the number allowed to pray in this fashion at any given gathering. Finally, in order to reinforce his instruction that the charisms should in their exercise be an expression of love and seek to benefit the entire community, he insists that praying in tongues be done in silence at the meetings, unless someone is present with the gift of interpreting the tongues to the rest of the community.

It would be a mistake, however, to regard Paul's restriction on tongue-speaking as a complete theology of this charismatic gift. There is, for instance, no hint in the letters to the Corinthians of the theology of glossolalia present in Acts. Paul is preoccupied with bringing order into a specific disorderly community whose members had apparently given scandal both to one another and to the pagan community among whom they lived. He is not, therefore, legislating for the universal Church. Moreover, he nowhere suggests that glossolalia is not a gift of the Spirit of God and he recognizes the gift as a form of prayer, as a way of "speaking to God" (1 Cor 14:28). These further reflections, however, yield two further insights into the charismatic experience.

2.4131 Every spiritual charism is given in order to be used as an expression of Christian love. Still, any spiritual gift once received can be perverted and abused if it is divorced from love (cf. 2 Cor 11:1-6).

2.4132 The use of charismatic gifts must be regulated by its beneficial effect upon the individual who possesses it and on the rest of the community.

There are two other significant aspects of the charismatic experience which can be gleaned from the first letter to the Corinthians.

3.51 The charismatic experience includes the hope of rising from the dead in the image of the risen Christ. Paul excoriates those in the community who deny the reality of the resurrection. He insists that the resurrection of Christ is a fact attested to by chosen witnesses and that it alone gives meaning to Christian baptism. Although the precise nature of the risen body remains mysterious, still it is through the spiritual transformation of his human flesh that Jesus has become the new Adam who communicates not merely terrestrial life to men, but the life-giving Spirit of God.

The very charismatic consciousness of the community is, therefore, a perpetual sign to it that Christ is truly risen and a pledge that it too is called to share in his resurrection (1 Cor 15:1-58; cf. 2 Cor 4:13-15; 5:14-15).

5. The charismatic experience is not the face-to-face vision of God. Paul warns the Corinthians that the light which comes through faith in Christ is imperfect; only in the next life will we be known as we are now known by him.

Study Guide Questions for Chapter 9

1. Why would these gifts fail to attract the public interest shown in the gifts discussed above?
2. What is your response to the position of some critics that the gifts of wisdom, faith, and knowledge are the property of all Christians after conversion, and thus not the result of the Baptism in the Holy Spirit?
3. How could a Spirit-filled believer share his gift of wisdom or prophecy without being considered pretentious or superior by fellow believers or nonbelievers?

10. Unique Features of Catholic Pentecostalism

Among the more amazing features of new Pentecostalism is the manner in which it has brought together Catholics and Protestants who only a decade ago were engaged in head-on theological disputation. Some Catholic observers see this as an unmixed blessing; others are enthusiastic but critical. Among the more important of the latter is J. Massingberd Ford, a member of the Theology Department at the University of Notre Dame, also a member of the charismatic community of that city. She has written two important works on this subject: Baptism of the Spirit: Three Essays on the Pentecostal Experience *(Techny, Ill.: Divine Word Publications, 1971), and* The Pentecostal Experience: A New Direction for American Catholics *(Paramus, N. J.: Paulist Press, 1970). The reader is also directed to the bibliography at the end of this handbook for information on the Catholic charismatic journal,* New Covenant.

This selection is helpful in that it deals directly with diocesan problems created by confusion over the new Pentecostalism.

Attitudes Toward the Institutional Church*

People sometimes suppose that the Pentecostal movement is anti-institutional, and that prayer meetings and other "esoteric" activities substitute for the liturgy and traditional Catholic devotions. Quite the opposite is true. The effect of the movement has generally been to give people a greater love and appreciation for all that is authentically traditional in the Church.

Among the earliest reports about the happenings at Duquesne was the increased devotion to the Eucharist that had resulted from them. The same was quickly verified at Notre

* Edward D. O'Connor, *The Pentecostal Movement in the Catholic Church* (Notre Dame: Ave Maria Press, 1971), pp. 166-71.

Dame, and has been confirmed by subsequent history. Nearly all those who take part in the prayer meetings attend Mass daily or at least frequently. What is more, many have commented on how much more meaningful the Mass has become for them. One student remarked that he had come to love the long lists of little-known saints in the old Roman canon, because the Eucharist meant so much to him that he was glad to summon all the angels and saints of heaven to join him in giving thanks for it.[1] When another student received the baptism in the Spirit, his first instinct upon returning to the University was to go to the chapel to give thanks. There he felt powerfully drawn toward the tabernacle by a force that seemed almost physical. The presence of Christ on the altar seemed to dominate the entire chapel, and draw everything toward itself. He spent an hour or more in wondering adoration before the Blessed Sacrament. Nothing of this sort had ever happened to him before.

Several persons have mentioned that the Holy Spirit has brought them a new sense of sin, and with it an awareness of the value of frequent confession, which they had neglected before.

Many have said they wished they could receive Confirmation all over again, now that they had so much more appreciation of the work of the Holy Spirit. It had meant little or nothing to them when they received it in their youth.

A Benedictine priest relates that the most striking effect of the baptism in the Spirit on him was that it gave him an eager desire to sing the Divine Office. Previously, this had been a burden; but now he felt a great longing to praise God, and the office was one of the most beautiful ways to do this. Other priests too have reported that the recitation of the office has become a joy for them.

---

[1] He made this remark without any awareness whatsoever of the criticisms of these lists that are being made by promoters of liturgical reform.

Devotion to Mary has been strengthened by the Pentecostal movement, not only at Notre Dame, as we have seen, but throughout the country. Some people, who had always been devoted to her, have rejoiced to find that the Holy Spirit has made her dearer than ever before. Many, whose devotion had been perfunctory or lukewarm, have become much more earnest about it, and in some cases have even become zealous promoters. A few, who used to experience a deep antipathy for Marian piety, now find that they can at least understand and accept it. (On the other hand, some of the "zealous promoters" have learned to be more tactful and understanding toward those who do not share their devotion.)

One couple tells how their prayer group gradually dwindled until only one other couple continued with them. Finally, at one meeting, the four of them sat in silence for an hour, just "listening" to what God might wish to speak. Then they decided to cultivate devotion to Mary. From that point on, the group began to grow larger.

After a prayer meeting at which prayers had been said for the bishops of the Church, a visiting priest commented wryly, "The Holy Spirit must be there. That was the first time I have heard anything good said about bishops in a long time!" Similar remarks have been heard several times. Although attitudes toward the clergy, and in particular the hierarchy, vary from person to person, and also from group to group, there is comparatively little of the anticlericalism or the tendency to deride and defy the bishops that is often so strong among energetic Catholic lay groups today.

Since a very early age, it has been recognized that obedience to those who hold office in the Church is one of the surest signs that an inspiration comes from God rather than from some secret craving of self-love. The Pentecostal movement has already been tested several times by this criterion.

In one diocese, the bishop gave orders to a newly formed

prayer group that there was to be no speaking in tongues or laying on of hands at their meetings. This came as a severe blow; there was considerable fear that these restrictions might bring the meetings to an end and cast a cloud of suspicion over the movement. Nevertheless, the group obeyed and, to their amazement, their numbers began to increase noticeably from that date onward. Furthermore, the restrictions themselves were lifted after a few months.

In another diocese, the prohibitions were even more severe. Besides speaking in tongues and the laying on of hands, exorcisms (even of an informal sort) and "asking for a text" (i.e., opening the Bible at random and reading whatever passages one chanced upon) were also forbidden at the prayer meetings. The only charismatic practice not forbidden was prophecy, and this was merely an oversight. Here again, the group submitted to the regulations of its pastors, and the fruits of this obedience were evident at once. At the very meeting at which the regulations were announced, the grace of prophecy was received for the first time in that group. The following day, one of those present sent the following account of the events in a letter to friends:

It's probably the best thing that has happened to us. . . . We had the best prayer meeting yet. . . . The Spirit was there in full, and we went away with a full harvest of love, joy, peace, patience, kindness, gentleness, and self-control. I'm saying this in real seriousness, because for me it was a real moment of closeness to Christ and filling with the Spirit. It was Christ overcoming the world. One of the things we felt was that this would be a call to seek the higher gifts, and sure enough we received prophecy for the first time. The two that we are sure of, and have written down are: "Bear in all patience what has happened to you. Obey those I have put over you. See the care I have for my flock." "Fear not, for the wonders I have worked among you shall not cease."

After a series of vicissitudes too complicated to be narrated here, this community was eventually allowed complete freedom in its prayer meetings. Meanwhile, it experienced a phenomenal growth, and became the instrument of God for bringing the gifts of the Spirit to an extraordinary number of people.

Not a few of those involved in the movement had previously been bitter critics of the Church. Some were vehement advocates of radical reform; others had given up hope of any improvement. There is at least one couple whose friends are surprised to find them still Catholic today, and another couple whose efforts to "enliven" parish life had met with such discouraging rebuffs from the pastor that they were on the point of abandoning the Church. The effect of Pentecost has been to restore their faith in the Church and awaken a new love for it. That some have remained in the Church is directly attributable to the movement. Those who made criticisms and advocated reform still do, but with less bitterness and more gentleness, patience and wisdom. No doubt, even in their fiercest moments, they have been animated by "zeal for the house of God"; nevertheless, it is a wonderful thing when the Holy Spirit, without argument or exchange of ideas, but simply by his warm and loving breath, imparts the insight that enables a person to perceive and be grateful for the mysterious, fecund holiness which he creates in the body of Christ despite its flaws, and to look upon the latter with understanding and compassion, rather than with the acrimony of a condemning judge.

Several priests and nuns who had been on the point of abandoning their state have had their hopes restored by the Pentecostal movement, and have determined to continue to serve the Church in their calling. One priest, a member of a religious order, had come to the generalate with the precise purpose of announcing his intention to leave. He had to wait two or three days before he could see the superior;

meanwhile, he observed such a change in the spirit of the men he knew there, as a result of the Pentecostal prayer meetings in which they were taking part, that when he did finally see the superior, it was to announce that he had changed his mind and was not going to leave after all.

No Instant Sanctity

Before we close the subject of the effects of the Pentecostal movement, two critical points concerning the suddenness and the durability of these effects must be discussed.

The foregoing pages have presented many instances of changes brought about quite abruptly. Moral and psychological bonds which a person had been unable to break in years of struggle have been lifted from him when he received the baptism in the Spirit. Graces of prayer and an appreciation of scripture quite incommensurable with anything in one's previous experience have been given in a moment.

These dramatic examples should not mislead us. The majority of spiritual developments, even among Pentecostals, take place quietly and gradually. Also when a given case is investigated, it often turns out that there has been more preparation than was evident at the moment. Looking back, one perceives that privileged moments of grace long ago had given him some foretaste of what was in store for him, or that suffering and anguish had been, in God's providence, sapping the walls of Jericho and getting them ready to fall.

But when due allowance is made for such factors, it still remains true that for a considerable number of people, the baptism in the Spirit has been a mighty intervention of the power of God in their lives, giving them suddenly and effortlessly results for which they had labored and prayed without success, and placing them many steps farther ahead on the road to sanctity than their previous progress would ever have entitled one to expect.

This is the summation of the movement within American Catholicism by one of its leading students.

Catholic Charismatics: A Critique*

It is at this point that many hear faint echoes of elitism. Are Catholic charismatics suffering from what Muriel Spark calls "chronic righteousness"? Do they speak from a great spiritual height to the unregenerated multitudes below? Undoubtedly such persons exist within the movement but they do not characterize it. Would Bishop Flores also be suffering from chronic righteousness? Further, the charismatics are not saying that Catholics in general have never effectively appropriated the basic Christian message. Rather they are saying this cannot be assumed even though it may later be shown to have taken place. Indeed from the programs at the national leaders' conference in Ann Arbor and the national convention at Notre Dame it is evident they are built on the supposition that many in the charismatic movement have not heard the basic kerygma effectively presented. The charismatics are attempting to go back and lay a solid doctinal foundation even for themselves in terms of a primary teaching: the meaning of salvation, sin, Christ as Lord, the kingdom of Christ, the demonic, walking in the Spirit, prayer, the Eucharist as community celebration of the resurrection, the church as the Body, community, service to others. These areas are expounded not as in a class of systematic theology, but as proclamation which elicits faith and commitment.

Where this emphasis on primary evangelization and a strong biblical-theological basis is lacking, there is a short burst of enthusiasm but no permanent growth. A number of instruments of teaching have developed, from short talks

* Kilian McDonnell, "Catholic Charismatics: A Critique," *Commonweal*, May 5, 1972, pp. 210-11.

for the curious, to seven-week introductory courses called "Life in the Spirit Seminars" for the more initiated, to twelve-week "Growth Seminars" for those already committed to the movement but in need of further teaching. These too are not purely a theological exposition, but a biblical proclamation in simple, personal, direct language, often done by a layman or woman for other lay people. And like the New Testament proclamation it is also an invitation to say "Jesus is Lord to the glory of the Father." In the large prayer groups and communities there are usually the personnel resources but in many of the smaller groups there are real problems finding teachers. Also in the small groups the programs of instruction are less ambitious.

That the most characteristic form of the Catholic movement is a prayer group or a covenant community is both a help and a hindrance. It helps because it gives a minimal structure within which the movement can grow and it provides mutual support. It hinders because the church as it now obtains is parish-oriented. As long as the charismatic groups are groups distinct from the parish, the movement cannot effect its goal which is to renew the whole church charismatically. Charismatics look at the parish with the same kind of ambivalent feelings as do others concerned with the renewal of the church. Many parishes simply need to die, while others can be real vehicles of renewal. Whether or not the parish is the ideal structure of the future, that is where the people are now, and that is where the charismatics meet the communities which need renewal. Unmistakably their aim is not simply to sanctify individuals but to transform communities. Therefore until the movement relates to the parish in other ways than through prayer groups the ideal of renewing the church charismatically will be an illusion.

There is nothing modest about the goal of the charismatic movement. Bert Ghezzi, George Martin and Kevin

Ranaghan have all spoken about the end of the charismatic movement as being comparable to the end of the liturgical movement. Ghezzi wrote: "The Pentecostal movement can cease to exist when everyone in the church is experiencing a full life in the Spirit. . . . The universal church has appropriated the renewal of liturgy which only a decade ago was the concern of a minority of enthusiasts. The liturgical movement no longer exists as a separate movement within the church, because the church has undergone a liturgical renewal." The goal of the charismatic movement is not to import the movement into the church where it will be tolerated. Rather its end is a church which is renewed charismatically and no longer needs a separate movement.

One might rightly have reservations about certain aspects of the movement but from a theological perspective it would be difficult to fault a movement which defines itself and what it desires for the church as "fullness of life in the Holy Spirit, the exercise of the gifts of the Spirit, directed toward the proclamation that Jesus is Lord, to the glory of the Father." . . .

The attitude of the bishops has greatly helped its growth. The first reaction of the bishops was astonishment and skepticism. By November 1969 there was enough positive evidence for the American bishops to give out a cautious but essentially positive evaluation of the movement, the first such to come from any American non-Pentecostal denomination. Two Presbyterian churches have since issued more extensive evaluations, also essentially positive. Today the general attitude of the bishops seems to be even more positive. The September issue of *New Covenant,* a monthly magazine published at Ann Arbor for the Catholic movement, printed positive evaluations by three North American bishops. Bishop Joseph McKinney, the auxiliary of Grand Rapids, is personally involved in the movement. A study group on the spirituality of priests sponsored by the American bishops has among its membership priests from the charismatic movement: Frank McNutt and Daniel Danielson. Bishop Arthur J. O'Neill, of Rockford, Ill., has allowed Father William McMahon to give up his parish and form a floating parish of a charismatic character. Written into the charter of the parish will be the stipulation that it will not own property.

An attempt has been made to indicate the reasons for its growth and ostensibly it grows because it has strengths. There are also weaknesses. Both the meetings at Ann Arbor and Notre Dame have seminars on the relation of the charismatic movement to social and political involvement. When at the 1971 national convention Father Harold Cohen asked for charismatic participation in the Catholic Interracial Conference to be held in New Orleans, his remarks drew loud applause. However, this aspect of the movement is not well thought-out and implemented.

Further, there is a kind of incipient dualism in some of the charismatic utterances. One can find isolated instances in which charismatics have sought rebaptism. Though there is general agreement among Catholics that it is not necessary to speak in tongues in order to be living the fullness of the life in the Spirit, some who hold such a doctrine teach that if you have not spoken in tongues you have not quite made it. Father Edward O'Connor has spoken out forcibly, as he always does, against this view. The borrowing from classical Pentecostalism (typified by the old-time Pentecostal churches) and from Protestant charismatics has been excessive and far too uncritical, sometimes in those areas where classical charismatics and those influenced by them are weakest, namely exegesis and systematic theology. Before it is too late, the Catholic charismatics have to rethink the charismatic spirituality within the broad framework of the Catholic tradition. Arnold Bittlinger, a Lutheran, and Robert Stamps, a Methodist, have urged this point.

These weaknesses are, to a greater or lesser degree, recognized by the national leadership, which is both sensitive and competent. Though priests are everywhere in evidence, though the national advisory board of the movement is about half clerical in composition, the movement is predominantly lay in orientation and in language. Many of the talks at national and regional meetings are given by laymen. At all levels laymen are exercising real pastoral functions. The clerical mind may find this alarming, and it might even seem highly clerical to say that one is impressed by the spiritual depth and pastoral skill of lay leaders. There are enough checks built into communities to serve as safeguards against unwise pastoral approaches, and most groups have some kind of priestly participation. In Catholicism, as in other branches of the movement in the other churches, the large role of the laity greatly contributes to its growth.

From the United States the movement is spreading to Mexico, Costa Rica, Peru, Brazil, New Zealand, Australia, England, and there are three prayer groups in Rome. In some places, France for instance, priests tend to be amused by reports coming from the States, as though one, after all, expects that sort of thing from Americans. Even in France there is much interest, though no sizable involvement. In most other countries, the movement is small but given the present patterns one can predict it will continue to grow. Assuredly it brings its own peculiar problems, but it could be a major force for renewal in the church.

Study Guide Questions for Chapter 10

1. Why might most American Catholics be more reluctant to explore the new Pentecostalism than most American Protestants?
2. Would Catholics be surrendering their traditional loyalty to tradition and clerical leadership by absorbing the major thrust of the new Pentecostalism?

11. The Communal Movement Within New Pentecostalism

Although few in number, several communal groups are emerging across the country based on the members' loyalty to their new faith in charismatic gifts. Little is known about these groups since they prefer anonymity. The theology underpinning the Catholic communal experiments is discussed in two books: Kevin and Dorothy Ranaghan, eds., As the Spirit Leads Us *(Paramus, N. J.: Paulist Newman Press, 1971), pp. 145-86, and Ralph Martin,* Unless the Lord Build the House . . . The Church and the New Pentecost *(Notre Dame, Ind.: Ave Maria Press, 1971), pp. 35-49.*

The selections presented here are brief descriptions of communal living among new Pentecostalists. Undoubtedly many more variations could be included, if we had ready access to learn about their whereabouts.

This is a brief selection about a well-established community which draws its inspiration from the charismatic renewal. The authors, Professor Luther P. Gerlach of the Anthropology Department at the University of Minnesota and Professor Virginia H. Hine, then his principal research associate, have published widely in the field of Pentecostal studies.

Living by Faith in Community*

Pentecostal commitment sometimes leads to a more subtle type of departure from cultural patterns, one that still involves a certain degree of risk. Many Pentecostals practice a form of financing called "living on faith." This means following the directives of the Holy Spirit as they are perceived

---

* From *People, Power, Change: Movements of Social Transformation* by Luther P. Gerlach and Virginia H. Hine, copyright © 1970, by The Bobbs-Merrill Company, Inc., reprinted by permission of the publisher.

in prayer, and depending upon what secularists would call "chance" to provide the necessary funds. Several of our informants depend for their entire support and that of their families on this type of supernatural control of ordinary business transactions. One of the tenets of this kind of faith is that "the Lord meets your needs, not your greeds." This involves a freewheeling capacity to change directions at a moment's notice. Long-range planning is not popular with those who live on faith. The Lord seldom allows the security of pre-planned budgets. If a need is not met, it means that the Lord has something else in mind for the believer to want. However, there is little value placed on austerity for its own sake. Unexpected luxuries are welcomed and enjoyed guiltlessly.

One group of Neo-Pentecostals, devoted to a charismatic ex-Lutheran minister, has been led by the Spirit to combine their families and their resources and to live communally, following the example of the first Christians. At the time of our research there were thirty people living in this "ministry center," four families with children and several single adults. Most adults spend full time going out to teach home Bible study groups, witnessing, and bringing people to the Baptism of the Holy Spirit. They were thus full-time recruiters for the movement. They did not expect their converts to join the communal group. Rather, they encouraged them to continue in their own churches, to spread the word, and to come to the weekly meetings at the center for spiritual refreshment.

The group relies for food, clothing, and shelter on the earning power of a few who work at their usual vocations. One of these is a doctor. The building which shelters them is a monument to the technique of faith financing. It is an immense, magnificent home built in the gracious style of the early 1900s. The leader of the group explains that the Lord directed him in a vision to acquire this home and its

147

spacious grounds. The Lord also provided the initial payments in the form of gifts from well-situated admirers of the leaders. Faith is put to the test each month when the mortgage payment comes due. The combined earning power of the group does not guarantee this amount, so that fairly substantial and practical answers to group prayer are constantly required. Sometimes these come in the form of unsolicited gifts from people who attend meetings and healing services held in the home. Sometimes a bit of bush-beating by the leader is required. But always there is the sense of spontaneity, of risk, and of reliance on something other than the usual patterns of economic security. This reliance has been successful for a period of four years.

The following selection is about the well-known community of charismatics in Houston.

Families and Community Life*

I suppose my wife and I had been married approximately 20 years when I received the baptism of the Spirit. When we started coming together in terms of community, our family was well along the way in terms of years. Several of our children were already teenagers. Each of the other four families also had several children and the parents were people of approximately our age at the time—between 35-40 years old. One of them was our pastor, Graham Pulkingham, rector of the Church of the Redeemer. He had been there for a year before all of these things started happening. Another was a doctor, Dr. Ekhart, a very successful general practitioner practicing about 35 miles from Houston. He had two offices in small towns and he was regarded as one

* Originally published in *New Covenant*, monthly magazine serving the charismatic renewal in the Catholic Church; P. O. Box 102, Ann Arbor, Mich. 48107. Reprinted with permission.

of the up-and-coming young physicians of the area. Another was an engineeer, Ladd Fields, who had been involved in a very technical kind of instrument field work for many years. And then there was a crew chief of a line crew for the power company, John Grimmet. He had worked for the power company for 25 years. All of us had families and we were all well-established people.

Very shortly after Esther received the baptism of the Spirit, I came across Graham. We discovered we had both been baptized in the Spirit and immediately started sharing. At that time Graham had been baptized in the Spirit exactly 30 days; me, for 18 months. The other men of the five families received the baptism of the Spirit just about that time and we began to gather together. The Lord put within our hearts an urgency to be together. We could see how precisely the Spirit of the Lord had picked us from the places where we were and chosen us to be a part of this particular undertaking. Very soon after we came together we began to get a sense about what the Lord was doing. He would encourage us. Practically anything we would pray for was answered almost instantly. It seemed impossible to get anything but a miraculous answer to prayer. All kinds of wild things would happen in our lives.

Moving Together

When the Lord began to speak to us about moving together into the neighborhood of the church, we were well prepared. For months we had been living a life that was shared in every way possible except geographically. By that time all our families were ready. The children were hungry for the life in the Lord. Our wives were sharing everything the men were sharing and they were a part of our gatherings whenever possible. Very often we would get free of our obligations and we'd get in the car and we'd run up to

149

Houston to the church or over to Dr. Ekhart's home. When we got there, we'd all pull our Bibles out and sit around the kitchen table or something like that and just start sharing what the Lord had been showing us and what had been happening in our personal lives. And you know, we'd just be awed at his majesty and grace, and we couldn't get over what he was doing to us.

I took several months to turn over files and things I was handling to my law partners and give up my law practice. Dr. Ekhart closed out his medical practice. Ladd and John kept working in their jobs because they were near their work, but we all moved right into the neighborhood of the church. Any house we could get that was close was suitable. We hardly worried what it looked like. We all came from big, beautiful homes but that didn't matter anymore. We were there to share our life in the Lord. We had such anticipation. It was just like a kid on Christmas Eve; we were expecting anything. We didn't know what we were going to do. We just knew we were supposed to be there and we were supposed to be together in serving the Lord.

I began looking for a job, trusting that the Lord was going to give me some work. For three months I diligently looked in all places I ought to be looking, but I did not find anything. There were no jobs opening up. After a while I said, "Okay Lord, you know what you're doing." So I started doing a little work out at the house, things that people would bring to me but it wasn't much. Mostly I just spend time helping Graham with the things that he needed.

At that time, troubled people were already coming to the church. The word had gotten around that the Church of the Redeemer was a place where people could get help. The day we moved into our house, we were joined by a confirmed alcoholic and a man who had spent most of the previous five years in mental hospitals. The day we moved in they moved in. Within another week, another mental case who was also an epileptic moved in. Then we got one or two younger men who were not really sick but who had just come to the Lord, been baptized in the Spirit, and needed to grow and be nurtured. Within no time at all seven other people were added to our household.

We started right away to live a community life. The men lived upstairs with my two older sons. The rest of the children, my wife and I, lived downstairs. We all ate together and we shared together. It was a community from the day we moved in. This was true of the other houses too. It was just the natural thing to do. People would come with needs and we'd know they couldn't be helped unless we took them right into our lives. We'd say, "Come on over and live with us and believe the Lord with us." The Lord honored that beautifully. He was just so obviously pleased. When one of the mental cases would get violent we would ask the Lord to do something, and the Lord would miraculously do something immediately. There were several times when one fellow went completely out of his head and we asked the Lord to restrain him. Immediately the man was restrained against a chair or on the floor and couldn't move; he was literally bound there like an angel was holding him down or something. We wouldn't touch him. He'd just be riveted to a chair or to the floor. We would see the powerful working of God's hand in those things and it encouraged us to ask him for impossible things.

Sharing Resources

Soon we naturally began to share our resources and to support people in our homes who had no resources or finances of their own. It became natural to share whenever anyone had a need. When somebody needed some furniture we'd share our furniture; if somebody needed a car we'd turn over our car to them. From the very beginning we began to share our possessions.

It soon became obvious that the needs we were faced with would take lots of resources and so we began to cut expenses for things we had been accustomed to. We stopped buying new cars and new televisions and things of that sort. We didn't even think of them. We became interested in these possessions just for their utility value. We started driving our cars until they literally fell apart and then we'd buy a used car or something like that to replace it. We began to turn in some of our insurances policies so that they would not be such a financial drain on us. We found such a security in our relationship with the Lord that it was no longer important to have security for the future or protection against this or that and so eventually we gave up most of our insurance policies except something like liability insurance for our cars that we felt we should have. We never have had any rule about it or a feel that this is a necessary part of the Christian life. It was just a matter of using the money we had available most effectively, particularly in supporting so many extra people. We learned to live very economically. We quit eating steaks and expensive roasts and things like that and we began to eat simple fare. We found that when simple food is properly prepared it is pretty tasty. We'd often eat things that people would bring to us. People would bring us a box of groceries or a hundred pound sack of rice, or they would bring us a washing machine. Sometimes somebody would bring a hundred pounds of fish.

Study Guide Questions for Chapter 11

1. Are these communes faithful to the form of communal living created at the first Pentecost?
2. Might the rapid spread of these kinds of communes pose a threat to such basic American economic institutions as insurance companies and banks?

3. Do you think such close living in a house among several families would most likely create more problems in interpersonal conflict than it would solve?
4. Would you want to live in a community such as those explained here? Why or why not?

12. What the Churches Can Do

Since the new Pentecostalism seeks to work within the main-line denominations, it is appropriate to conclude this hand-book with suggestions on how the participants and the church bodies might draw on each other's strengths and, in turn, avoid the pitfalls made by old Pentecostalists and older mainliners in the past. The bibliography has specific information on which church offices have documents available for distribution on the new Pentecostalism. This selection, prepared in 1970 by a com-mission of the United Presbyterian Church in the United States of America, serves as an excellent set of directions for the future of the movement.

Guidelines*

We believe the Church needs to pray for a sensitivity to see the manifestations of the Holy Spirit in our world today. We are not unmindful that the problems of discrimination between the true and the fraudulent are considerable, but we must not allow the problems to paralyze our awareness to his presence, nor should we permit our fear of the un-known and the unfamiliar to close our minds against being surprised by grace. We know the misuse of mystical experi-ence is an ever-present possibility, but that is no reason to preclude its appropriate use. We believe that those who are newly endowed with gifts and perceptions of the Spirit have an enthusiasm and joy to give and we also believe that those who rejoice in our traditions of having all things done in "decency and order" [Editor's Note: a cherished Presbyterian teaching] have a sobering depth to give. We therefore plead for a mutuality of respect and affection.

* Report of the Special Committee on the Work of the Holy Spirit.

The criteria by which we judge the validity of another's religious experience must ever be its compatibility with the mind and spirit of our Lord Jesus Christ, as we know them in the New Testament. If the consequence and quality of a reported encounter of the Holy Spirit be manifestly conducive to division, self-righteousness, hostility, exaggerated claims of knowledge and power, then the experience is subject to serious question. However, when the experience clearly results in new dimensions of faith, joy, and blessings to others, we must conclude that this is "what the Lord hath done" and offer him our praise.

Guidelines for All

1. Be tolerant and accepting of those whose Christian experiences differ from your own.
2. Continually undergird and envelop all discussions, conferences, meetings, and persons in prayer.
3. Be open to new ways in which God by his Spirit may be speaking to the Church.
4. Recognize that even though spiritual gifts may be abused, this does not mean that they should be prohibited.
5. Remember that like other new movements in church history, Neo-Pentecostalism may have a valid contribution to make to the ecumenical Church.

Bibliography

Space limitations prohibit the inclusion of a complete bibliography here. Four kinds of information, presented below, may be helpful for further reading on both general and specialized subjects.

I. *Materials from New Pentecostal Sources*

Several publishing houses and centers for information deal exclusively with new Pentecostal materials, including books, tapes, filmstrips, and tracts.

Logos International
185 North Avenue
Plainfield, N.J. 07060

Christian Growth Ministries
Box 306
Ft. Lauderdale, Fla. 32203

Whitaker Books
504 Laurel Drive
Monroeville, Pa. 15146

Ave Maria Press
Notre Dame
Notre Dame, Ind. 46556

Wachtung Book Service
P.O. Box 292
Wachtung, N.J. 07061

Society for Pentecostal Studies
Box 122
Franklin Springs, Ga. 30639

The *Logos Journal* may be obtained by subscription from Logos International.
New Covenant is available by subscription from Box 102, Main St. Station, Ann Arbor, Mich. 48107.

II. *Critical Interpretations*

These books, not all of which were used in this handbook, have excellent bibliographies.

Bruner, Frederick Dale. *A Theology of the Holy Spirit: The Pentecostal Experience and the New Testament Witness.* Grand Rapids: Wm. B. Eerdmans Co., 1970.
Durasoff, Steve. *Bright Wind of the Spirit: Pentecostalism Today.* Englewood Cliffs, N.J.: Prentice-Hall, 1973.
Gerlach, Luther P. and Hine, Virginia H. *People, Power,*

Change: Movements of Social Transformation. Indianapolis: The Bobbs Merrill Co., 1970.

Hoekema, Anthony A. *Holy Spirit Baptism.* Grand Rapids: Wm. B. Eerdmans Co., 1972.

————.*What About Tongue Speaking?* Grand Rapids: Wm. B. Eerdmans Co., 1966.

Hollenweger, Walter J. *The Pentecostals: The Charismatic Movement in the Churches.* Minneapolis: Augsburg Publishing House, 1972.

Kelsey, Morton T. *Healing and Christianity in Ancient Thought and Modern Times.* New York: Harper & Row, 1973.

Kildahl, John P. *The Psychology of Speaking in Tongues.* New York: Harper & Row, 1972.

Nichol, John Thomas. *Pentecostalism.* Plainfield, N.J.: Logos Books, 1972.

O'Connor, Edward D. *The Pentecostal Movement in the Catholic Church.* Notre Dame: Ave Maria Press, 1971.

Ranaghan, Kevin, and Ranaghan, Dorothy. *Catholic Pentecostals.* Paramus, N.J.: Paulist Press, 1969.

Samarin, William J. *Tongues of Men and Angels: The Religious Language of Pentecostalism.* New York: The Macmillan Co., 1972.

Synan, Vinson. *The Holiness-Pentecostal Movement in the United States.* Grand Rapids: Wm. B. Eerdmans Co., 1971.

Unger, Merrill F. *New Testament Teaching on Tongues.* Grand Rapids: Kregel Publications, 1971.

III. *Other Books on the New Pentecostalism*

Basham, Don. *Deliver Us from Evil.* Washington Depot, Conn.: Chosen Books, 1972.

Bennett, Dennis J. *Nine O'Clock in the Morning.* Plainfield, N.J.: Logos International, 1970.

Bixler, Russell. *It Can Happen to Anybody.* Monroeville, Pa.: Banner Publishing, 1970.

Boone, Pat. *A New Song.* Carol Stream, Ill.: Creation House, 1970.

Carothers, Merlin. *Power in Praise.* Plainfield, N.J.: Logos International, 1972.

————. *Prison to Praise.* Plainfield, N.J.: Logos International, 1970.

Kuhlman, Kathryn. *God Can Do It Again*. Englewood Cliffs, N.J.: Prentice-Hall, 1969.
———. *I Believe in Miracles*. New York: Pyramid, 1968.
Larson, Bruce. *Ask Me to Dance*. Waco, Tex.: Word Books, 1972.
———. *Dare to Live Now*. Grand Rapids: Zondervan, 1967.
———. *Living on the Growing Edge*. Grand Rapids: Zondervan, 1971.
Martin, Ralph. *Unless the Lord Build the House*. Notre Dame, Ind.: Ave Maria Press.
Roberts, Oral. *The Call: Oral Roberts: Autobiography*. New York: Avon Books, 1973.
Saint, Phil. *Amazing Saints*. Plainfield, N.J.: Logos International, 1972.
Seamands, John T. *On Tiptoe with Joy*. Atlanta: Lay Renewal Publications, 1971.
———. *On Tiptoe with Love*. Kansas City, Mo.: Beacon Hill Press, 1971.
Sherrill, John. *They Speak with Other Tongues*. New York: Pyramid, 1964.
Shoemaker, Sam. *Under New Management*. Grand Rapids: Zondervan, 1971.
———. *With the Holy Spirit and with Fire*. Waco, Tex.: Word Books, 1972.
Stott, John R. W. *The Baptism and Fullness of the Holy Spirit*. Downers Grove, Ill.: Inter-Varsity Press, 1964.
Walker, Alan. *Breakthrough: Rediscovery of the Holy Spirit*. Nashville: Abingdon Press, 1969.
Wilkerson, David. *The Cross and the Switchblade*. New York: Pyramid, 1968.
———. *The Jesus Walk*. Old Tappan, N.J.: Fleming H. Revell, 1972.
———. *Life on the Edge of Time*. Old Tappan, N.J.: Fleming H. Revell, 1972.
———. *One Way to Where?* Glendale, Calif.: Regal Books, 1972.
———. *Promises to Live By*. Glendale, Calif.: Regal Books, 1972.
———. *Purple Violet Squish*. Grand Rapids: Zondervan, 1970.
———. *When in Doubt . . . Faith It*. Glendale, Calif.: Regal Books, 1970.

IV. *Official Denominational Statements*

Several of the large church bodies have published helpful studies of new Pentecostalism for general distribution. These are:

A Report on Glossolalia, 1962. The American Lutheran Church, 422 South Fifth St., Minneapolis, Minn. 55415.

Preliminary Report, Study Commission on Glossolalia, The Episcopal Church, Diocese of California, 1055 Taylor St., San Francisco, Calif. 94108.

Report of the Committee on Doctrine of the National Conference of Catholic Bishops, 1969, reprinted in O'Connor, *The Pentecostal Movement in the Catholic Church*, pp. 291-93.

Report of the Special Committee on the Work of the Holy Spirit, The United Presbyterian Church in the United States of America, Witherspoon Building, Philadelphia, Pa. 19107.

"The Person and Work of the Holy Spirit," 1971, The Presbyterian Church in the United States (out of print). Copies may be available from Office of Information, Columbia Theological Seminary, Decatur, Ga. 30031.